# Fighting for Public Services

Better Lives, a Better World

# Fighting for Public Services

## Better Lives, a Better World

Fritz Keller and Andreas Höferl

Public Services International

First published 2007 by Public Services International
45 avenue Voltaire, 01210 Ferney-Voltaire, France

www.world-psi.org

British Library Cataloguing in Publication Data
A catalogue record for this book is available from the British Library


ISBN-10 0 7453 2706 0
ISBN-13 978 0 7453 2706 8

HD
8005
.K455
2007

Designed and produced for Public Services International by
Chase Publishing Services Ltd, Sidmouth, EX10 9QG, England
Printed and bound in the European Union

# Contents

Appendices:

# Preface

Public Services International (PSI) is the global federation for public sector trade unions. It will be celebrating its centennial at its congress on 24–28 September 2007 in Vienna, Austria. When planning for the congress started in 2002, it was agreed that PSI should commission a history book.

However, it was also agreed that a book that contained only the history of the organisation itself would short-change the organisation: the knowledge of where a union body has come from is important but it was felt that it was also important to know the kinds of struggles that had led to the development of public services, irrespective of the work of PSI.

How and why did municipal governments in Europe in the late nineteenth century – often relatively conservative governments – decide either to establish public services for their citizens or to take over the ownership and running of such services from private sector operators? That is a very relevant question 100 years later, after a few decades in which their successors, as well as national governments and intergovernmental bodies such as the World Bank and the International Monetary Fund have been moving in the opposite direction, often 'selling' these services to their friends and allies in what are mainly multinational companies. What do those very different late nineteenth- and late twentieth-century experiments tell public sector trade unionists and users of public services about what is possible, what is a threat and what we need to do?

So, the decision was made to commission Fritz Keller and Andreas Höferl to attempt to do both of these things.

In Part One, Fritz Keller, a respected Austrian labour historian, working in association with the Austrian Association for Policy Consulting and Development, takes us through the history of PSI. His approach has been to look at the major political events of the twentieth century, with a view to seeing what kinds of challenges these presented to PSI and its affiliated unions. How did PSI and public sector unions respond to the two world wars, to the rise of fascism, the challenges of the Cold War, the potential offered in national independence struggles in the developing countries emerging from Northern colonialism?

Who were the key players – both personally and organisationally? Who were PSI's allies and who were its foes? How did it move from being a federation of European municipal/utility unions, completely dominated by men, into an organisation whose membership is now mainly female and whose affiliates are mainly in the South? (Although this latter point should not be used to hide the fact that politically and financially, the reality of power residing in the North has not substantially changed over the century that has passed.)

Part Two describes the history of public services worldwide, such as health and social services, pensions, water and sewerage, waste management, gas and electricity, police, security and culture. Many of these services evolved as a result of the rapid growth of urban communities in the nineteenth century. The principle of public service provision was so successful that it was adopted very quickly in developed cities, especially in Europe, and remained in place throughout the twentieth century, notwithstanding massive political and historical changes. In the post-war era in particular, public service provision contributed substantially to unprecedented economic growth and wealth creation. The past decades of liberalisation and privatisation of public services are full of examples of how the private sector market forces alone fail to secure efficiency and equity.

Andreas Höferl (Chapters 7, 8, 9 and 16) is a historian and political advisor in Austria. He and his co-authors Werner T. Bauer (Chapters 11, 13 and 14), Bela Hollos (Chapters 10 and 12), Michael D. Huber (Chapter 16), Patricia Schnarr (Chapters 7 and 9) and Luise Wernisch (Chapter 15) work for the Austrian Association for Policy Consulting and Development. Since 2002 they have published several studies about privatisation and liberalisation of public services in the European Union (find out more at <www.politikberatung.or.at>).

One of the more difficult decisions in producing the book was the question of graphics. We could have used a mixture of mainly modern photos and old photos/prints. However, it was realised that it would be virtually impossible to find a representative range of such material that avoided the fact of little of it being available from the early years and most of it being from the North. Most union photo archives also tend to focus on 'famous' people and/or meetings – neither of which displays well the action that is central to union activism.

We therefore opted for two sets of graphics: those of Austrian artist Otto Rudolf Schatz on labour and working-class activism in the Europe of the first half of the century; and those of José Venturelli Eade, the Chilean artist whose 1980s Latin American work for PSI is from a later period and a different place.

Reprints of the woodcuts of Otto Rudolf Schatz are thanks to the permission of the copyright owners, Prof. Michael Jursa and Dr Martin Jursa (both from Vienna, Austria). The prints appear on pages 2, 4, 22, 72, 148, 156, 164, 170, 184, 186 and 194. None of these woodcuts or any part of them may be reproduced, stored in a retrieval system, or transmitted in any form or by any means, electronic, electrical, chemical, mechanical, optical, photocopying, recording or otherwise, without the prior permission of the copyright owners.

José Venturelli's prints belong to PSI, since we commissioned them from the artist in 1985. They appear on pages ii, vi, x and xii.

In both cases, biographical details of the artists are to be found in Appendices B and C.

Hans Engelberts, PSI General Secretary since 1981, has a wealth of knowledge about the most recent quarter of a century of PSI, a time during which many of the most significant developments and challenges have occurred, especially with the official ending of the Cold War. He has been able to comment on many parts of the text where archives have been of little use.

In fact, archives have been one of the problems confronting the exercise: as Fritz shows, PSI was 'chased' from Germany, then The Netherlands and then France and then to London during the Second World War. Inevitably, archives were not on the top of everyone's packing list priorities in these dangerous times and almost all PSI archives of the first 40 years have been lost.

Philip Smith translated Part One. Sabine Huebler translated Part Two. Our thanks to both of them.

A note is needed about the resource material used for this book. It was decided from the beginning that we did not want to put off general readers who might be intimidated by academic-looking footnotes and references. But knowledge of these resources is important to other researchers. In Appendix D, a resource guide for the book, there is both a discussion about the resources used and an indication as to where they can all be found on-line.

Thanks are also due to three PSI staff who helped in the research exercise entailed in tracing the name changes that early affiliates have undergone. In many cases, it took some detective work to find the modern names, where they exist, of unions from the early parts of the twentieth century. Veronika Darras, Gabriela Caruso and Catherine Bond were the bloodhounds who found all the traces.

We should thank Mike Waghorne, PSI Assistant General Secretary, who essentially managed the project, tying together all the loose ends, getting the package into its final shape and liaising with our friends at Pluto Press and Chase Publishing Services.

But, of course, from PSI's perspective, most thanks have to go to the members and officers of all of our affiliates, whose struggles and ideas have been so crucial in building and defending the public services that make PSI possible. Those who have gone before us have many things to teach us and we hope that those yet to come will find inspiration and commitment in this book to continue those struggles.

Fritz Keller
Andreas Höferl
Hans Engelberts
January 2007

# Part One

## A Century of the Global Union Federation for Public Service Workers: Public Services International: 1907–2007[*]

* The original text for this publication was written in German. In some cases, references and quotations were produced in German, often from another original language. In many of these cases, the original language version cannot be located and so has been retranslated from the German.

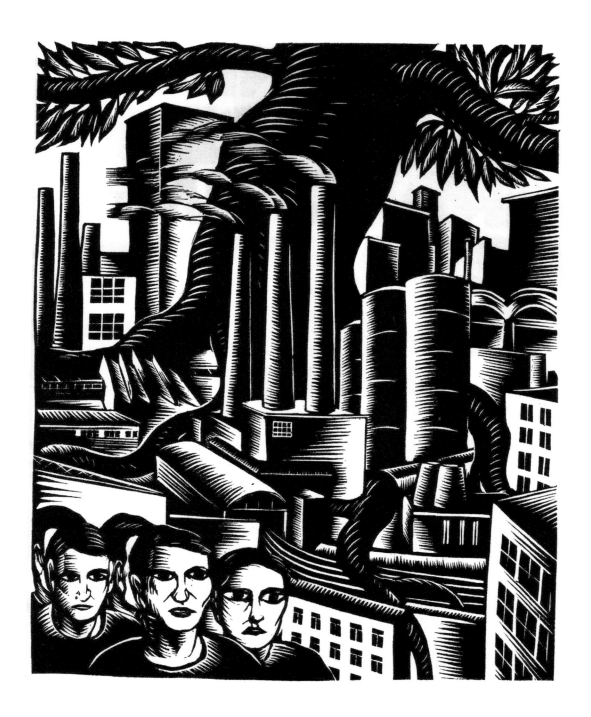

# Introduction

The early part of PSI's celebrated 'golden age' fired the imagination of many activists because it held out the promise of better things to come. The creation of municipal socialism by public servants in projects like 'Red Geneva', Labour-run Sheffield or 'Red Vienna' appeared to create a modern utopia in the 1920s and 1930s. After the destruction wrought by fascism and the Second World War, the Nordic model of 'prosperity for all' was introduced for the first time in human history in all industrialised countries. Even the developing world appeared to be at a historical turning point that offered a way out of the vicious circle of poverty.

Today the wholesale dismantling of public services and social security systems that are part of the neoliberal onslaught illustrates that PSI faces issues that hark back to the early days of capitalism. This goes hand in hand with constant brainwashing that makes people believe that there is no alternative to the corporate drive for globalisation, that we must face the challenges of competition, whatever the cost. Despite this propaganda there is nothing inevitable about 793 dollar billionaires – they are worth over US$2.6 trillion, which is more than what the poorer half of the world population owns. And frequent parroting by neoliberal fundamentalists does not make Margaret Thatcher's platitude that 'there is no alternative' any more accurate.

Consider the following: the Nordic countries still have a high level of trade union organisation, collective bargaining and public services of exemplary quality, for which people are willing to pay higher taxes; despite this the World Bank places them at the top of the list of national economies when it comes to their competitiveness: Finland comes first, Sweden comes third, Denmark fifth, Norway sixth and Iceland tenth.

*'Another world is possible!'\** The 640 unions (148 in Africa and Arab-speaking countries; 134 in Asia–Pacific; 141 in Inter–America, and 217 in Europe) with 20 million organised public services workers in 154 countries want to contribute to its creation.

Hans Engelberts
PSI General Secretary

---

\* The slogan of the general movement of civil society organised around the World Social Movement in its various annual forums.

# 1

# The Foundation Age

The upper ten thousand* in their grand first-floor apartments in the properties built by the early industrialists heaved a sigh of relief in 1907: the threat of all-out war between the industrialised nations could be confined to a bloody altercation between Russia and Japan. A new session of The Hague Peace Conference had put its seal on the new coexistence in Europe by updating the rules pertaining to war on land and at sea. Rebellious Hottentots, Algerian Berber tribes, Persians, Palestinians, rebels in the USA's South American backyard, and Chinese military auxiliaries trained by foreign instructors – any who refused absolute obedience could still simply be crushed.

On the social front the situation justified the bankers' and factory and mine owners' cautious optimism: hadn't the mass strikes and protests in the oil fields of Baku, St Petersburg and Germany's Ruhr petered out? Well-organised miners had been able to squeeze out some concessions in return: in Britain, the eight-hour day for miners under 18; in France, a reduction of working time to nine hours underground; in Germany, a government promise to improve working time, health conditions and the internal disciplinary system. But what did such pledges matter whilst capitalism's expansionist period lasted, as long as the steam turbines kept the wheels of industry turning, as long as business and profit grew without limit? The upper ten thousand continued to luxuriate in a lifestyle that was a never-ending 'Waltz Dream', after the Oscar Strauss operetta.

Those who lived on the lower floors, the sub-letters or those who paid only for a bed in the tenements on the outskirts of the city, were a ready audience for different words and tunes: 'Arise, ye workers from your slumber.' Taking control of your own life, closing ranks with fellow-sufferers, standing up for shared interests, even going on strike, had all proven themselves a success.

---

* 'The upper ten thousand' is a common German-language term to refer to capitalists and powerful people.

Throughout Europe, trade unions were established in new sectors of the economy – most were organised by members of social democratic parties, but some set up by Christian socialist or even nationalist activists.

The social democrats within this growing network of solidarity were vehemently opposed to any nationalism because it jeopardised trade union cooperation across borders. 'The International unites the human race.' They therefore organised an International Socialist Congress in Stuttgart from 18–24 August 1907. The event began with a multicultural event involving 60,000 people at a fairground. In a familiar ritual the delegates condemned any form of colonialism of 'foreign lands … and peoples … brutally exploited for the benefit of a small minority'. The trade unions that made the economic arguments and the political parties who dealt with political disputes should work closely together to 'free the proletariat from the bonds of intellectual, political and economic slavery'.

All socialist Members of Parliament in all countries wanted to introduce simultaneously bills in their respective parliaments for statutory restriction of the working day. Realising that pan-European carnage had been only narrowly avoided, 'workers and their parliamentary representatives are obliged to mobilise so as to use all available means to prevent the outbreak of war'. 'If, however, war were to break out', it was decided 'to exploit the economic and political crisis the war causes to shake up the social classes and hasten the downfall of capitalist class rule'.

A few days after the International Socialist Congress, a meeting was held from 25–27 August 1907 in the Green Room of the Trade Union Centre in Stuttgart of the 'employees of council and state institutions in power, light and water works, as well as those employed in nursing and hospitals', their first international conference. These groups of public sector employees had kept a low profile for a long time, despite their frequently poor working conditions. In fact, municipal facilities and offices were often turned into workplaces more resembling parade grounds for military square-bashing, and the pay of messengers, office workers, road sweepers and lamp lighters was barely higher than the paltry welfare paid to the poor. All this had been accepted for decades in the hope of a job for life. But then the population that acquired a right to voice its opinion at town and municipal level due to advances in democracy was less willing to accept the serious shortcomings in meeting people's basic needs because of business owners putting profit first:

- toll attendants on bridges
- fire brigades, which were funded by the insurance companies and mainly rescued the property of their clients in the town centre but happily left the outskirts to be consumed by the flames
- graveyards, the cost of which was horrendous and which escaped all health regulations
- hospitals run by charities and poor committees that resembled army barracks
- competing gas companies that even in London's Oxford Street installed two parallel gas pipes, both of which were of such poor quality that a quarter of the gas leaked out
- abattoirs that sold tubercular meat
- horse-drawn transport that used decrepit horses, filthy carriages and poorly paid staff, and which did not serve the poorer parts of town
- water companies that were only concerned with supplying water to the affluent parts of town and who were happy for the poor to continue fetching water from contaminated wells and springs (even at night they did not fill the existing pipes with sufficient water, and this caused a catastrophe if a fire broke out).

City administrations were still firmly in the hands of the liberal parties, and they had been forced to take into common ownership first the water, gas and electricity companies, and later other utilities, because of these inadequacies and above all because of the pressure on the budget caused by the cost exacted by suppliers now operating in merged international companies. The city of Glasgow was an example, where a comprehensive system of public ownership was established as early as 1890 and it included companies that built workers' housing, libraries, a sewage treatment plant, docks in the harbour, an electricity generator and street lighting, mains water, a milk depot for nursing babies that was subject to health inspection, museums and art galleries, parks and gardens, public baths and a telephone company. Industrialised countries throughout Europe followed this trend – often by incurring huge debt in the form of loans.

The number of public employees rose so sharply with the advent of communal services that critics feared 'city workers would be able to tyrannise society through their vote'. In reality it was the liberal or conservative City Fathers who tyrannised their 'civil servants' and they happily creamed off the healthy profits with the same insouciance as any shareholder. 'Work in city companies is always harder, dirtier and more dangerous than in most private industries.' 'Wages' were not at all 'attractive to workers from private industry' and pension entitlements were in some cases below the level of welfare to the poor, concluded a survey carried out about 'The Conditions of Municipal Workers in Germany'.

Organising workers in the public sector had started in Britain, which at the time was the centre of the world economy. As early as 1888, activists (men and women) of what would become the Gas Workers' Union (now GMB*) had brought production to a halt in Beckton – and they had the support of Karl Marx's daughter Eleanor and her husband Edward Aveling. The Danes, Swedes, Norwegians, Germans, Hungarians, Dutch and Swiss followed suit. Generally the relatively well-paid gas workers were the vanguard – driven by their working conditions: 12- or sometimes 18- and even 24-hour shifts; farm labourers, exposed, unprotected from all weathers, when working outside; furnace workers grafting in temperatures of 40–70 degrees (Celsius) and everywhere dust and noxious gases. As the vanguard, the gas workers had not only suffered at the hands of the police, the army and firemen trying to break strikes, but had been the first victims of the transnational companies that inevitably grew out of competition, such as the Dessau Gasworks with branches as far afield as Finland, Russia, Sweden, Norway and Hungary, or the London-based Imperial Continental Gas Association with offshoots in Germany, France, Italy and Denmark, or the internationally active Saxony-Thuringia Gas Company with its headquarters in Leipzig. The multinationals brazenly played off the workers

---

*   The union was founded in 1889 as the National Union of Gasworkers and General Labourers. In 1916 it became the National Union of General Workers and in 1921 absorbed the National Federation of Women Workers. In 1924 it amalgamated with the National Amalgamated Union of Labour and the Municipal Employees' Association to form the National Union of General and Municipal Workers. Since 1982 it has been the General, Municipal, Boilermakers and Allied Trade Union, known only as GMB.

in their different locations and if necessary used their corporate network to recruit strike breakers.

By 1907, several international trade secretariats existed in some sectors: there was even an international secretariat of national trade union federations for global coordination of national federations. Now an international group of workers from the water and electricity sectors and from municipal administrations was to be brought into this network. Some of the unions of allied trades who feared they could lose members resisted the move. But the delegates at the Stuttgart congress agreed. Their shared pledge to uphold the unreserved right to organise and strike caused no problem either. Opinions differed widely when it came to putting these ideas into practice: the initiator of the meeting, Albin Mohs from Berlin, wanted to 'paint the strike in the sky like a black ghost, but if possible never use it because municipal workers should instead increase their political influence and so improve their conditions'.

A Hungarian delegate reported on the successful use of passive resistance. 'People work but less gas is produced, but as people are working nobody sends for the army.' The French even considered sabotaging production as a weapon in the struggle, but the Dutch representative dismissed it as 'French cant' and the German delegates 'rule it out simply because of the effect on public opinion'. The Hungarian delegates, however, did not think it possible to influence public opinion 'because our factories are prepared to spend one hundred thousand a year to influence the press'. The debate also illustrates the big differences in status between different public workers. Whilst in Germany those who ran communal companies would have liked to bring pay levels down for the organised workers to below the private sector, the Svenska Kommunalarbetareförbundet (Kommunal) (Swedish Municipal Workers Union) was an integral part of the factory workers' federation and its members were paid the same wages as other workers. The Danish municipal workers were 95 per cent unionised and were members of Dansk Arbejdsmandsforbund (Danish Workers Union) and had been able to forge ahead in terms of pay compared with the private sector.

The Danish, German, Dutch, Swedish, Swiss and Hungarian delegates approved a general resolution at the end of the conference on behalf of over 44,000 members that covered 'right of assembly and right to

strike', 'pay and working conditions' 'general workers' welfare provision' and against 'immoderate consumption of alcohol'. The chairman of the Arbeiter- und Staatsarbeiterverbandes (the German Workers and Public Workers Federation), Mohs, was appointed treasurer and given the task of the day-to-day running of the new Public Services International (PSI).*
The organisation faced its first test just weeks after the conference: striking Hungarian gas workers needed urgent support. PSI was able to send 500 marks through an emissary, to which the German workers added another 1,000 marks from their own funds.

Again straight after the Socialist Congress in Copenhagen, from 4–6 September 1910 the next meeting of 30 representatives of public sector companies from ten federations and eight countries took place in Folkets Hus in Jagtvej 69. The meeting noted shortcomings in setting up an efficient information network because of a lack of funds. Nevertheless, the International Secretariat subsequently published a survey, 'The Wage and Working Conditions in Municipal Undertakings in Various Countries', that can be considered the pioneer of international comparative trade union statistics. The information for the survey had come from Belgium, Great Britain, Denmark, France, Germany, the Netherlands, Luxembourg, Norway, Austria, Sweden and Switzerland.

The Swedes managed to negotiate a total of 47 collective agreements, the Germans only five, but one of them – in Jena – went so far as to guarantee workers a seven-and-a-half-hour day. In the rest of Europe people generally worked ten hours a day, six days a week; in some exceptional cases people worked an eight-hour day, but only as part of a 24-hour shift system. The lamp lighters in Nuremberg worked a 16-hour day, and in water and electricity companies people worked around the clock. The working day of 12–15 hours in hospitals, nursing homes and sanatoria made for a high turnover of staff. Overtime was standard practice, but being paid for it wasn't. Bonuses for working nights, Sundays and public holidays were rare indeed. Employees at the gas works generally earned more than street cleaners; French and Scandinavian workers earned more than their Belgian

---

\* The name of what is now called 'Public Services International' has changed throughout the years (see Appendix A). Unless needing to refer to a specific title, we will use 'Public Services International' or 'PSI' when referring to the continuing organisation, to avoid confusion.

and German counterparts. Top earners (men and women) got nine marks a day, which was just about enough to support a family of four. The average wage was between three and a half and five marks. Nevertheless, thanks to new technology human labour was replaced wherever possible with new methods (tilt loader for alembics, water gas plants) to save money and to reduce the 'likelihood of strikes', as bluntly reported in the *Journal for Gas Lighting*.

The Austrian municipal workers were in such financial straits that the next meeting planned for Vienna in 1913 had to be moved to Zurich. In the People's House (Volkshaus) on Helvetiaplatz, eleven trade unions from ten countries that represented 102,900 members took stock and sounded a cautiously optimistic note: 'The trade unions of the state and municipal workers have won respect in their countries.' French delegates from the Féderation Nationale des Travailleurs Municipaux et Départementaux* (National Federation of Municipal and Departmental Workers) vehemently demanded 'campaigning for general and simultaneous disarmament in all countries', which was rejected by fifteen votes to seven. However, a list of demands that was akin to a manifesto was accepted. It was to be given final approval by the affiliated unions at the next conference:

- The recognition of trade unions and their representatives for negotiating pay and working conditions.
- Settlement of pay and working conditions in a collective agreement.
- The eight–hour day and related rest periods amounting to 36 hours per week.
- Sufficient pay that is exemplary in terms of amount, type and payment, weekly wage payment, payment for holidays that fall during the working week.
- Restriction of overtime and holiday work to what is absolutely necessary.
- Appropriate notice of dismissal, protection against dismissal for illness or accident, job protection against arbitrary dismissal.

---

* It has not been possible to trace with certainty the history or development of this union as it has changed its name over time. This is the case for many other unions named in this history, often as a result of the loss of records during one or another war.

- Mediation tribunal comprising representatives of the employers and the employees under independent chairman for work related disputes.
- Sufficient health precautions, provision of work clothes, provision of hygienically clean huts and toilets for building workers.
- A summer holiday on full pay, continued payment of wage for minor absences, military service, illness or accidents.

# 2

# The First World War and its Aftermath

From 1 July 1914, PSI was able to provide a salary to its secretary, Albin Mohs, for the first time. But just one month later, Oscar Strauss' *Chocolate Soldier* (playing at playing soldiers) moved from the opera stage to the battlefields of Ypres, Isonzo, Verdun, Langemarck and the Somme. The German federation immediately concluded that 'without doubt the world war had destroyed the conditions required for an independent international secretariat'. However, Mohs was able to mobilise five of the ten affiliated organisations (Belgium, Denmark, the Netherlands, Luxembourg and Sweden) to support continuation of the International Secretariat. He worked to prevent the friendly contacts with the officials of the Belgian Association des Ouvriers des Différents Services Publics de la Ville et des Communes de l'Agglomération Bruxelloise (Association of Public Services Workers of Brussels and the Surrounding Municipalities) and the Dutch Bond van Nederlandsche Gemeentewerklieden (Union of Dutch Municipal Service Workers) from being destroyed, and campaigned – in vain – for deported Belgian workers.

## The First Peace?

In the autumn of 1918, 7.9 million lay dead on the battlefields and the world of the bourgeoisie was in ruins. The trade unions all had to start afresh after being brought into the war effort nearly everywhere for their 'fatherland'. The International Secretariat, which had been renamed the 'International Trade Union Federation', convened for this purpose two meetings of delegates from 16 countries in Amsterdam. In the aftermath, the International Secretariat of the Workers in Public Services reorganised at a meeting in October 1919. A formal constitution was approved for the first time. Mohs, as the only official, had to be jack-of-all-trades, and he played an important integrator role in getting the Verbandes der Gemeinde- und Staatsarbeiter Deutschland (German Federation of Municipal and State Workers) back into the international community, which was now dominated by representatives of the victorious powers; the International Secretariat moved from Berlin to Amsterdam.

Then came the start of close cooperation with the International Labour Organisation (ILO), an offshoot of the League of Nations that had been established according to ideals of US President Woodrow Wilson. 'Universal and lasting peace can be established only if it is based upon social justice', it says in the preamble to the ILO Constitution. Fighting unemployment and the introduction of the eight-hour day were urgent objectives. They were to be introduced by means of the moral pressure of conventions and recommendations brought together in an international body of labour law.

Governments now sat at the table with employers and workers' representatives at the ILO – including public service trade unions – as both sides of industry grew more confident in their ability to reach settlement by negotiation. They felt that clear signals had been sent out during the war in the form of control of the food supply, price setting by government, introduction of a cereal monopoly, municipal food supply and the creation of new welfare facilities.

Could the state apparatus, that had started to judder, be taken over from the inside and the communally owned parts of the economy put at the service of 'municipal socialism' or some other kind of welfare state? 'Civil service, this most decent and gracious of arts, because its action affects living people, is based upon melding state and people into one economic and spiritual unity in which all members carry within them the awareness of this belonging as an irremovable possession', it says in the journal of the Verbandes der Gemeinde- und Staatsarbeiter Deutschland. At a PSI congress, the representative of the International Federation of Labour, when addressing the General Secretary of the International Transport Workers Federation, Edo Fimmen, was even more forthright: 'Our task must not be limited to improving the conditions in our own trade, but put at the service of the great freedom struggle of the working class.'

Such hopes and the short post-war boom at first brought a huge rise in membership amongst non-manual workers from the civil service that had swollen because of the arms industry and social measures taken, as well as the employees of public law corporations and institutions. Non-manual workers started to dominate the public service unions: at the end of 1921 PSI already had 484,112 members. However, things came back down to earth in 1925. At the congress held in the Magistrates Meeting Room in Berlin Town Hall, delegates took stock: 'Despite the League of Nations and the Peace Pact, expenditure on militarisation … has increased hugely. Unemployment and short-time work are the key features of most industrial countries, so we can talk of a real failure of the capitalist regime. Reactionary influence is most noticeable in the area of removing business from municipal ownership', but working time was also under attack: Mussolini increased standard working time in fascist Italy to nine hours a day.

## Crisis

The economy was caught in a lengthy and depressive downturn and refused to pick up. Unskilled workers built machines on an assembly line driven by an electric motor, and this allowed the general introduction of systems that standardised the labour force and working time (Fordism or Taylorism). Average profit margins dropped. To attempt a reorganisation of state finance, governments took their lead from orthodox economic liberalism (priority given to currency and price stability) by dismantling social systems and dismissing workers, combined with anti-union legislation.

In Britain, for example, a Conservative cabinet passed the Trade Disputes and Trade Unions Act 1927, prohibiting general and sympathy strikes and strike pickets, and prohibiting trade unions in the public sector from joining the national trade union federation or the Labour Party. It made the trade unions liable for damage done during disputes, and so on. The Labour government which was in power from 1929 to 1931 did not repeal this 'strike breakers' charter'. Their spokesmen called for 'appropriate' pay and also claimed that the financial superpower of the day that was based on sterling could go bankrupt because of the cost of the unemployed. Like all other governments of industrial countries, Labour did not want to hear about budget reorganisation by means of nationalisation of the private arms industry as a step on the way to complete disarmament, as advocated by PSI. Despite this adversity, PSI membership climbed to 599,290 by 1931.

Meanwhile, US President Edgar Hoover set out to balance the budget using the usual economically liberal methods. The central bank reduced credit: Congress declared a trade war, leading to a series of bank collapses and a huge stock market crash. During Wall Street's black days after 24 October 1929, speculators gambled wealth that had been created by workers' hands over many years – US$50 billion in total. The army of the unemployed grew vastly. Hunger was again a daily occurrence in all industrial countries, whilst farmers hoarded their produce and coffee was burned to power trains, to keep the world market price high.

'*Before Sunset*'* (Gerhart Hauptmann). The internal discussions that took place at the PSI Congress in 1932 about how to deal with the world economic crisis were summarised under the slogan 'Fight for the public economy'. The 'public sector is at least equal in status to the private sector' because 'it accomplished tasks of a wide-ranging and social nature in the interest of the broad mass of the population'. Even more so as 'private business operated by individual entrepreneurs are clearly ceding more and more to the cartel and monopoly economy run by "civil servants"'. More specifically, the delegates called for:

1. nationalisation of mining, heavy industry, the energy sector and passenger and goods transport …
2. reform of the banking and credit system with a view to its nationalisation. To this end central banking offices are to be created in individual states. Their task will be to run a single banking and credit policy in the interest of the national economy
3. rehabilitation of the world economy and resolution of the world economic crisis can only happen through planning and management of the economy.

---

* Throughout, the author has used references to song titles to indicate a theme he wishes to emphasise. 'Before sunset' reflects the moment before the close, before the sun goes down – a moment to be sung, danced to, swayed to, shared – just in time.

Factory workers were called on to achieve as quickly as possible 'effective control' over hiring and firing, the 40-hour, five-day week; overtime was to be scrapped as workers would instead be given time off in lieu. Anyone unable to find work should receive as high an unemployment benefit as possible.

These demands were reflected in a series of ILO meetings that dealt with public service issues such as:

- 1928 and 1931: questions regarding working hours and holidays
- 1930: maternity leave
- 1931 and 1933: current municipal workers' pay.

ILO conventions covering these matters were subsequently agreed.

## The Special Nordic Path

ILO conventions were only really put into practice in Scandinavia. Here the social structures that had been established by free and equal farmers had long paved the way for extraordinary social developments. As early as 1886, for example, the trade unions in Denmark, Norway and Sweden had agreed to cooperate closely following a congress in Gothenburg. And in Denmark in about 1900, the only trade union of its time that was made up entirely of women from all imaginable professions and trades was founded, Kvindeligt Arbejderforbund i Danmark (Women Workers Union of Denmark).* Strong fascism was absent in Scandinavia – there were only small right-wing extremist groups that were supported from abroad.

In the 1930s, work was therefore rationed in Denmark according to the ideas shared by the Dansk Kommunalarbeiderforbund (Danish Union of Municipal Employees) and people were generally on compulsory 'short-time' work days and overtime was compensated by time off in lieu. In 1933, an entitlement to unemployment benefit was enshrined in law and subsequently support was given to cultural facilities for the unemployed,

---

* This union merged with the Specialarbejderförbundet I Danmark (SiD) (General Workers Union of Denmark) in 2005 to form Fagligt Faelles Forbund (3F) (United Federation of Danish Workers).

such as workers' universities, and so on. In 1936, the White Collar Workers' Law provided protection from dismissal and, in 1938, the Holiday Law stipulated at least two weeks' holiday a year. In Norway, the trade union federation – of which the PSI affiliate Norsk Kommuneforbund* was a member – and the Labour Party established the Workers' Crisis Demands (better job security, laws on old-age pension and unemployment insurance) that were introduced by the social democratic government that ruled from 1935.

The Swedish trade union confederation – of which Svenska Kommunalarbetareförbundet (Kommunal) was a member – worked with the Social Democratic Party, that formed the government over decades from 1932 onwards, on developing a model for development of a 'people's home' (folkhemmet), the name given to the welfare state, that in many ways anticipated the theories that were to be developed in later years by the economist John Maynard Keynes. In 1938, the trade unions and employers concluded a general work agreement. In 1939, the Riksdag passed a law prohibiting the dismissal of women because of pregnancy, childbirth or marriage. Thanks to these measures productivity rose quickly to the level it had been before the world economic crisis.


## Amid Fascism ...


Outside the Nordic countries, the atmosphere of impending economic and political disaster unleashed forces bent upon snatching power from the shaky grasp of the upper ten thousand with brute force. Benito Mussolini and his blackshirts were the first with their march on Rome in 1924. A year later, the Italian member organisation of PSI was absorbed into the fascist Federazioni – and at its congress in 1925, PSI promised 'its broadest support to the workers in public services and companies in Italy in their fight to win back freedom of expression and assembly'.

Adolf Hitler's assumption of power in January 1933 caused the loss of the Verband der Gemeinde- und Staatsarbeiter with its 393,000 members.

---

* The predecessor of today's Fagforbundet (Norwegian Union of Municipal and General Workers).

The PSI secretariat had moved to Schlesische Strasse 42 and then to Michaelkirchplatz in Berlin after the public sector workers had merged with the Arbeiter der Gärtnereien und des Deutschen Verkehrsverbundes (the Gardening Workers and German Transport Federation) and it now had to be evacuated quickly to Amsterdam and later Paris. A stand-in secretary undertook this move during March and April 1933. The PSI secretary, Fritz Müntner, had been thrown out of his flat and expelled by his colleagues from the German organisation as an 'enemy of the state'; he was a sick man and died in April 1933 of a heart attack at the age of 63.

Simultaneously, the trade secretariats of the building workers, assistant hairdressers, hotel, restaurant and cafe workers, hat makers, ceramic workers, agricultural labourers, painters, machinists, heating engineers, shoe and leather workers and tobacco workers fled Nazi Germany. None of the trade union support facilities, particularly the International Mateotti Fund, was able to withstand the onslaught. The countries that border Hitler's Germany helped as best they could: the Danes treated refugees from the Third Reich as their own unemployed and in addition made a contribution to travel costs. People from the Saarland in Germany had a similar experience because they were supported in their work by funds from the Schweizerischer Verband des Personals Öffentlicher Dienste (VPÖD, the Swiss Federation of Public Service Employees*), which was unused money of their own refugee support fund.

The International Federation of Labour was at first not even able to give PSI office space. All the activities were run from a private flat, with even typewriters and duplicating machines on loan. Finally, the efforts to get the Nazis to release PSI funds were successful. The funds were in the form of 25,000 marks in debentures from the Hannover Bodenkredit Bank, 11,000 in certificates of the Königsberg Reichsmark loan and 17,000 Reichsmark in Prussian mortgage bonds. This was enough to secure continued publication of the international bulletin – the French version was printed and the German, English and Danish editions duplicated in the office.

The financial problems lessened only slightly when the International Federation of Labour provided PSI with an office in its own premises for an

---

* This union has two other official names: in French, the Syndicat suisse des services publics (SSP) and in Italian, the Sindacato svizzero dei servizi pubblici.

annual rent of just 3,000 francs. The main problem was that the shortfall in the finances caused by membership dropping to fewer than 300,000 could not be made good. As if the situation were not bad enough, the member organisations also had to cope with a shortage of funds. For example, the Irish Transport and General Workers Union* was unable to pay its dues and was therefore expelled.

And the fascist advance in Europe continued: as a consequence of the attempted Austrian workers' uprising in February 1934 the victorious Austrian fascists outlawed the public workers' organisation. The Czechoslovak Samospravnych Státnich a verejnych ch zamestnancu Ustredni svaz (Central Union of Self-governing State and Public Employees) in Prague, the Federation of Public Workers in Liberec and the Polish Zwiazek Procownicow Instytucy Uzytecznosci Publiczey (Trade Union of Employees of Public Service Institutions) were Hitler's next victims. The Spanish Federación de los Trabajadores de Gas y Electricidad (Federation of Gas and Electricity Workers) succumbed to General Franco after the defeat of the Republicans in the civil war.

## ... and Communism

On another front, PSI was constantly forced to deal with attempts by the communists who were in power in the Soviet Union to use the revolutionary wave that emanated from the First World War to establish a system of global workers' councils. The October Revolution exercised considerable power over members and officials, particularly among German municipal and state workers. Nevertheless, PSI rejected the application of the Russian public workers' organisation at its conference in 1923 following the decisions of the International Federation of Labour. Sometimes there was agreement to break the (shaky) united front with the communists, as happened during the protest campaign against the French occupation of the Saar in 1923. However, this anti-communist leaning did not prevent member organisations or individual members from taking part in events

* In 1990 it was part of a merger to form the Services, Industrial, Professional & Technical Union (SIPTU).

organised by the Krasnyi Internatsional Profsoyuzov (Profintern) (the Red Trade Union International. In practice, PSI and the International Federation of Labour tried to roll back communist influence, mainly by taking a pragmatic attitude.

The longer fascism's onward march lasted in Europe, the stronger the drive for unity at all levels. After 1931 there were greater attempts to organise international cooperation between the public and municipal workers, postal workers, civil servants and teachers. At the same time, PSI attempted to strengthen the mutual loyalty of individual professional groups through international conferences. Examples of this are the meeting of the gas, water and electricity workers in Kiel and the meeting of health professionals in Bern.

In 1935, the rivalry between PSI and the International Federation of State Workers and Teachers was set aside and they united. This merger had the potential to make a political rapprochement with the communists easier, as they had officially abjured plans for world revolution in favour of cooperating with social democrats and even with the bourgeois liberals as part of a broad front against fascism. The shared commitment to the Republican side in the Spanish civil war provided a clear illustration of that cooperation.

However, within PSI, an overwhelming majority rejected even study visits to Moscow. The communists, with their blind devotion to Stalin, repeatedly upset any potential partners: for example, when they destroyed all the Bolshevik old guard in the Moscow show trials; then their campaign of terror, against the anarchists and Trotskyists who were fighting on the side of the Spanish Republic, that they unleashed just a few weeks after a big solidarity conference in London, which had also been attended by PSI delegates; and finally through the Hitler–Stalin pact to divide Poland.

# 3

# From the Second World War to the Golden Age

After the collapse of the Spanish Republic, the PSI secretary, Charles Laurent, attended a series of meetings between the board of the International Federation of Labour and the international trade secretariats: aid to the refugees had to be coordinated and preparations made for an international trade union congress. The meeting was held on 5–8 July 1939, after which an international conference of gas and electricity workers took place in Zurich in 1939. Soon the whole of Europe rang to the sound of the marching songs of the brown-shirted soldiers: a Nazi song went 'We shall march on when all is dust and shards, today we rule over Germans, tomorrow the rest of the world' (*Wir werden weiter marschieren, wenn alles in Scherben fällt, denn heute gehört uns Deutschland und morgen die ganze Welt*).

On 9 April 1940, Hitler's army crossed the border into Denmark without any declaration of war and a day later it landed in neutral Norway. The PSI members Dansk Kommunalarbeiderforbund (the Danish and Norwegian Unions of Municipal Employees) and Norsk Kommuneforbund attempted – as did all other trade unions in both countries – to coexist with Nazi occupiers, but this attempt finally failed in September 1940 and on 29 August 1943, respectively.

'*We shall march on*'. On 10 May the Nazi army attacked the neutral countries Belgium, The Netherlands and Luxembourg – PSI members the Union Centrale Belge des Travailleurs des Services Publics (now the Centrale Générale des Services Publics (CGSP) – Belgian Central Union of Public Service Workers) and the Nederlandsche Bond van Personeel in Overheidsdienst (Dutch Federation of Government Service Personnel) also fell victim.

'*We shall march on!*' On 14 June, German units goosestepped up the Champs Élysées to the Arc de Triomphe. Nearby, in the Palais Bourbon district, where the PSI offices were housed in rue de Solferino 10, Secretary Charles Laurent hurriedly destroyed all important documents. The Nazi commanders took away the surviving documents, many of which disappeared from the international office, never to be seen again.

When the Germans occupied Paris, PSI – which had been able to transfer £2,092 to London before the occupation – formally suspended its activities until just after the end of the war. Representatives from PSI and four other trade secretariats, however, participated in a committee established in London by the International Federation of Labour, from which an Emergency International Trade Union Council was established in 1942.

Within this structure, PSI activists continued their discussions about socialist manifestos and theories of economic planning. Subjects covered included the New Deal Programme launched by US President Franklin D. Roosevelt (it established working time and minimum wages, introduced unemployment insurance for the first time, accident and pension programmes, state-run job creation programmes such as the Tennessee Valley Project), as well as the social reforms brought in during and just after the war by the British Labour Party (extensive nationalisation, a health service that did not involve an insurance component, modernising the education system).

In parallel with this preparatory work for rebuilding the labour movement, PSI activists played an important role in supporting resistance groups during the war. They were imbued with the belief that had been described at the PSI conference back in 1936 with the words: 'Our friends under dictatorships shall arise and take the place that is their due.'

The toll taken by the Second World War was appalling: one third of the Jewish people murdered in a bestial, atrocious and brutish manner; the upper echelons of the labour movement snuffed out; 30,225,570 dead soldiers, 24,840,000 dead civilians, 35,000,000 wounded; uncounted numbers uprooted and driven out, and the atomic clouds over Hiroshima and Nagasaki were the writing on the wall for the survivors …

## A Second Peace?

During the military conflict, it had been easy for the USA to modernise and vastly extend its means of production. All other capitalist states were considerably in debt to the USA. As after the First World War, a US President, this time Franklin D. Roosevelt, set out the global economic and military principles: under US leadership, 26 allies – the United Nations – pledged, on 1 January 1942, to continue the war against the Axis powers until they unconditionally surrendered. On 26 June 1945, the United Nations succeeded the ailing League of Nations. Its founding charter promises the establishment of an economic and social council to resolve international economic, social and cultural problems. (Although the actual power to act was already in the hands of multinational companies and the Bretton Woods institutions that acted in their interest, such as the World Bank and the International Monetary Fund.)

Part of this emerging post-war order was to be a new world trade union federation that built upon the anti-fascist struggle. The idea was for it to grow out of the Anglo-Soviet Trade Union Committee that had been set up after the German attack on Russia – albeit without the involvement of any trade secretariats. After exploratory talks with the two wings of the American labour movement, the World Trade Union Congress was held in London on 6–17 February 1945. The Congress of Industrial Organisations attended the meeting but the American Federation of Labor categorically refused to cooperate because of the participation of communists.

The 63 trade union federations and 13 internationals (including PSI) in the City Hall representing nearly 60 million members from 46 countries were united by the hope of a new beginning that avoided the mistakes made between the world wars. At the first congress from 25 September to 10 October in Paris, the statutes, a charter of fundamental trade union rights and a statement on reconstruction were approved. PSI had a provisional secretariat at 5 Endsleigh Gardens and sent four delegates, including the secretary-designate, Maarten Bolle, from the Nederlandsche Bond van Personeel in Overheidsdienst. A meeting of the reactivated PSI Executive had approved this step on 2 September.

The Executive's decision was that the secretariat, which had in the interim moved to 119 Oxford Street, should call delegates to an ordinary conference on 28–30 May in the Zurich Kongresshaus. There were twelve member organisations, including the United Public Workers of America, meaning a non-European union was represented for the first time. On behalf of 1.3 million members the delegates approved a programme that contained social demands linking back to pre-war demands (full rights of organisation, monthly pay, bonuses for working on Sundays and holidays and at night, full sickness pay, sufficient pensions). There was a new call for joint decision-making with management (earlier this had been known as worker control). The overall goals of the World Federation of Trade Unions (WFTU) were recognised by PSI as a common basis for action.

Behind the scenes within the WFTU, the conflict between, on one side, the communists and, on the other, the two American federations and the social democratic unions was growing. The first clash came over the role of trade secretariats – a discussion that had already been held in the International Federation of Labour without much success. PSI General Secretary Bolle became the spokesman of a kind of Counter-International to the communist-dominated WFTU. Critics claimed that the purpose of its exaggerated centralising tendencies was the creation of completely supine, impotent and subordinate organisations. To exert pressure on PSI, some of the members who were under communist influence stopped paying their dues. As a counter measure, PSI expelled the Czech Ust edni Rada Odború (Central Committee of Trade Unions), the Magyar Köztisz-tviselók es Közalkalmazottak Szakszervezete (Trade Union of Hungarian Public Officers and Servants), the Fédération Nationale de l'Éclairage et des Forces Motrices (National Federation of Public Lighting and Power Workers), the Fédération des Travailleurs de l'État (now the Fédération Nationale de Travailleurs de l'État/Confédération Générale du Travail (FNTE/CGT) – National Federation of State Workers/General Workers Confederation), the United Public Workers of America and the British National Union of Public Employees.

In the light of a second revolutionary wave (Yugoslavia, Greece, Vietnam, Korea, China, mass strikes in Italy and France), the USA, under the new Harry S. Truman government from the right of the Democratic

Party, moved from a policy of 'containment' through cooperation to one of 'rollback'. A generous European Recovery Programme was to help moderate politics gain ground in the whole Western hemisphere.

The WFTU rejected any discussion of the Marshall Plan. Resistance to US aid grew within PSI. The Civil Service and Clerical Association of Great Britain voted against the Marshall Plan at the PSI Executive Committee, because it saw it as a political plan, with provisions in bilateral treaties covering areas such as national policies on currency, interest rates, investment and foreign trade. Nevertheless, Trade Union Advisory Committees were set up to work on the implementation of the European Recovery Programme in those countries willing to accept American help – a measure which got the full support of the PSI Executive. The disputes within the WFTU escalated.

After the final breakdown of talks between the trade secretariats and the WFTU held in Paris on 14–16 September 1948, representatives of the American Congress of Industrial Organisations, the British Trades Union Congress and the Dutch Nederlands Verbond van Vakverenigingen (now the Federatie Nederlandse Vakbeweging (FNV) – Dutch Federation of Trade Unions) left the organisation at a meeting held on 17–19 January 1949 and founded – after preparatory talks that had been attended by Bolle representing PSI – the rival International Confederation of Free Trade Unions (ICFTU). Echoing what had previously happened between European governments, this concluded the clear split between East and West within the labour movement.

During the debates at the founding conference of the ICFTU in November and December 1949, Bolle insisted on keeping the traditional division of tasks: trade secretariats should continue to deal mainly with issues from their sector, the international organisations with political issues at world level. To clinch the argument, he pointed out that the trade secretariats had 2 million members in 25 different countries, yet the central union organisations had not joined the ICFTU. The delegates to a conference of the international trade secretariats held in The Hague from 27–28 May 1950 voted in support of this view and moreover gave 'unconditional and unanimous support to the view that they wanted to fight alongside the International Confederation of Free Trade Unions for the liberation and progress of workers around the world'. Bolle said that this fight was to be taken to 'final victory' (consciously copying the term used in Nazi propaganda). PSI, which now had a new secretariat at 67–69 Whitefield Street in London, had made its position perfectly clear.

# 4

# The Golden Age

The Cold War was at a critical phase: the ICFTU, with the help of its large organising machine of 72 people, called on its members to support the action taken by the UN Security Council against North Korea. Joseph R. McCarthy and his committee for un-American activities hunted alleged communists, including 1,456 government workers; Stalin and his followers staged show trials against alleged spies.

The atmosphere in society was increasingly conservative: the expert from the American Federation of State, Country and Municipal Employees (AFSCME) reported to a PSI meeting in Munich in 1953 on statutory strike bans in the public sector in New York, Michigan, Minnesota, Missouri, Nebraska, Ohio, Pennsylvania, Texas and Virginia. There was an extensive ban on policemen and policewomen joining a union, and such clauses were becoming more common in other work contracts ('yellow dog' contracts). Despite resistance from the All-Japan Prefectural and Municipal Workers Union (JICHIRO), the government passed a strike ban for the whole public sector, even covering workers within the tobacco monopoly. Civil servants generally lost their right to collective bargaining.

PSI protests were as ineffective as the new ILO conventions: the Freedom of Association and Protection of the Right to Organise (No. 87) and the Right to Organise and Bargain Collectively (No. 98). The long and expansionist upswing in the economy, built on the technological advances brought by semi-automation, was based on a social rollback to 'normality'. Nevertheless, many PSI members hoped for the adoption of the system used in the British public sector of Joint Industrial Councils comprising representatives of the trade unions and the employers. The task of the body was to find consensus between all participants to optimise production – using the following means:

- agreements covering pay, working time and working conditions
- health, safety and welfare measures
- creation of bodies for rapid settlement of disputes (arbitration boards)
- promotion of union membership
- representing the sector in talks with government, local and other authorities.

Measured against these expectations, the co-determination rights of PSI member unions remained limited at plant level and informal. To boost the professional profile of trade union officers in this area, PSI organised sector seminars for most professional groups that the members represented. Great importance was attached to attracting trade unionists from the rank and file:

- public service workers in state administrations at central government, federal, state and municipal levels
- social security workers
- hospital, health and social workers
- employees of publicly owned gas and electricity companies
- employees of other publicly owned companies
- employees in public transport
- firefighters
- police (men and women) and prison warders
- blue- and white-collar municipal workers
- blue- and white-collar workers in the nuclear and allied industries.

Special meetings were held to consider general trade union rights, as well as the particular problems facing shift workers in all sectors. A PSI General Council discussed a survey on the actual implementation of the 40-hour week in 1956. The agenda of the PSI congress of 1961 in Stuttgart covered bargaining rights, working time and the pensions of public sector workers.

PSI's growing commitment to individual sectors was influenced by the challenge coming from the activities of the competing Trade Unions

International of Public and Allied Employees, that had been launched in two well-publicised conferences of the communist-led WFTU in Vienna in 1955 and Leipzig in 1959. A PSI memo to unions seeking admission referred to this challenge as the 'battle for the minds of men that is now being fought by the forces marshalled on both sides of the iron curtain'.

PSI made considerable progress in obtaining representation in intergovernmental organisations: again the ILO was of particular practical value. In a statement made in Philadelphia on 10 May 1944, the ILO had set itself new and far-reaching goals: 'as long as poverty reigns, affluence is everywhere in danger', so a 'more intensive use of productive forces … through measures to extend production and consumption, to avoid cyclical variations, to promote economic and social progress in the least developed areas of the world' was required. PSI was usually invited as an observer to meetings of the ILO Advisory Committee on Salaried Employees and Professional Workers and was able to influence decisions of the ILO governing body through the ICFTU. The fruits of this lobbying can be found in ILO resolutions on

- public servants
- hospital and health service staff
- future action in the field of labour–management relations and
- an ILO experts committee on nurses.

PSI lent its moral support to all UN activities, as it had to its predecessor, the League of Nations. It sometimes obtained observer status at the organisation's Economic and Social Council. At the United Nations Educational, Scientific and Cultural Organisation (UNESCO), PSI acted as a link to member organisations in running international worker exchanges to promote education and international understanding. Its attempt to gain observer status at the World Health Organisation (WHO) failed because the WHO only wanted to admit organisations dealing exclusively with health issues (a refusal that stands even today, after several attempts).

The trade secretariat had links with the Organisation for European Economic Cooperation (which, in 1961, became the Organisation for Economic Cooperation and Development, OECD) that had been created by the countries involved in the Marshall Plan. Negotiations were held with the International Atomic Energy Agency over terms of employment in the state energy sector and a solution was agreed with all participating trade union federations.

The German philosopher Karl Jaspers mused about '*The atomic bomb and the future of humanity*': this was an issue on which PSI had to provide a reasoned response in the middle of the Cold War. Its congress was held in 1958 in conjunction with the Brussels World Exposition in the shadow of the 100-metre-high Atomium structure. Delegates called for universal disarmament through a major expansion of international law as set out in the UN charter and contained in decisions of the International Court of Justice. Given the risk of destruction of all civilisation, the delegates saw a ban on nuclear arms testing as a first step in that direction. The resolution was silent on the USA's announced strategy of massive nuclear retaliation and the declared rearmament of all North Atlantic Treaty Organisation (NATO) countries (including West Germany) with atomic weapons and missiles. A majority decision on unilateral disarmament within the British National Union of General and Municipal Employees sank without trace.

Despite these various international activities PSI remained centred on Western industrialised countries until the end of the 1950s: out of its eighteen paying members, only four were based outside Europe (one of which was the Union of Jewish Clerks and Office Workers); of the fifteen non-paying members, twelve were based in the Third World. General Secretary Maarten Bolle had made a first attempt to expand after the Second World War. He had accepted an invitation from the American Federation of Labor to attend their congress in Houston with the idea of using personal contacts to overcome their traditional lack of interest in international labour issues.

Subsequently, he travelled to the Far East and to regional conferences of the ICFTU and ILO in Asia. During his trips he contacted public service unions in Burma, Hong Kong, India, Japan, Malaysia, Singapore and Thailand, The General Secretary had wanted to use decolonisation to attract new members to PSI, to increase its standing in the long term among trade secretariats and with governments around the world. His ambitious plans, which were in line with the plans of the Socialist International to get a foothold in Asia, had been rejected by trade unionists in the (former) colonial powers, who in 'their' sphere of influence preferred the federations of the ICFTU, based on the nation state, to the supra-national structures of a trade secretariat. When representatives of the National Union of General and Municipal Employees refused to pay into the PSI solidarity fund, Maarten Bolle stoically tendered his resignation.

His ideas enjoyed something of a renaissance as the struggle for influence in the Third World between the two superpowers intensified. At the end of the 1950s, there was a crisis in Laos; the war in Indochina flared up again; in Indonesia – where nationalism was generally anti-capitalist because the Dutch controlled the plantations, the oil industry, mines, shipping, banks and wholesale trade – President Ahmad Sukarno was flirting with the communists; there was a civil war in Lebanon; the Syrian Baath party switched to the Soviet side; Yemen was in ferment; the Algerian liberation movement was on the brink of victory; in Ghana and Guinea, pro-communist regimes came to power; under Patrice Lumumba's leadership, the African liberation movement arrived in Belgian Congo; and Fidel Castro beat the Fulgencio Batista dictatorship in Cuba. Simultaneously worried and encouraged by the crisis brought about in Eastern Europe due to de-Stalinisation, the USA stepped up its counter-insurgency measures. PSI established another solidarity fund in March 1957.

The organisation claimed 5,000 members in Latin America at this time. Under the aegis of the American Federation of Labour and Congress of Industrial Organisations (AFL-CIO), therefore, a Western Hemisphere Conference of Public Servants was convened in Mexico in 1961 with the energetic support of the Federación de Sindicatos de Trabajadores al Servicio del Estado (Trade Union Federation of State Services Workers). The conference decided an extremely ambitious programme. In particular the conference called for the signature of ILO Conventions Nos 87 and 98 on trade unions rights and freedom to organise, areas where the local situation was not good (in Brazil, Venezuela and Peru, public service workers were banned from joining trade unions).

To attain these goals AFSCME made available to PSI a full Inter-American Office, including a representative and support staff. The funding came from the Gotham Foundation, based in a small New York lawyer's office. This 'PSI team' operated broadly as an agent of US foreign policy, including spectacular actions like investing £250,000 in bringing down the government of Castro-sympathiser Cheddi Jagan in the British colony of Guyana.

Its success in recruiting new members remained modest, however. The Inter-American Office had to close in 1964, once the international media had revealed its links with the CIA. Reacting to these events, the PSI General Secretary invited members in the region to make suggestions about how to continue the work. Only the Argentinian Confederación de Trabajadores Municipales (Confederation of Municipal Workers) responded with a development programme. Two years later, all PSI member organisations in Latin America had 128,000 members, according to their own sources (of which 70,000 were in Argentina).

In keeping with decisions of the ICFTU, President Adolph Kummernuss in 1958 headed a delegation which included, most importantly, officials of AFSCME who visited Tunisia, Libya, Sudan, Uganda, Kenya, Tanganyika, the two protectorates of the Central African Union (Northern Rhodesia and Nyasaland – now Malawi) in the white settler-dominated Southern Rhodesia (today Zimbabwe), Belgian Congo, Nigeria, Ghana, Guinea, Senegal and Morocco. There were at this time 21,867 members in the whole of Africa.

As modern industrial relations in Africa were restricted to the state administration and allied sectors, Kummernuss and his delegation wanted to canvas the possibility of recruiting more members in this sector to stop the 'Bolshevik penetration and the subsequent stealthy conquest of the continent for the doctrine under the symbol of the hammer and sickle'. Their findings were sobering: nearly all organisations south of the Sahara had low or unverifiable membership figures; the union premises looked extremely pitiful; and the officials were under the influence of the colonial regimes and feudal structures, and were often unaware of the union's aims and not at all steadfast in their convictions.

To stabilise the situation, PSI sent experienced European officials with financial resources to Tanganyika, Nigeria, Uganda, Zanzibar, Kenya and Aden. Finally, the post of 'special envoy' was created to represent the General Secretary in the field; this support was available at any time as a kind of trade union development aid. This assistance was targeted towards direct recruitment of new members to PSI, but was from the outset considered unworkable in the French-speaking countries (Senegal, Ivory Coast, Niger, Dahomey, Cameroon, Congo Brazzaville and Congo Leopoldville). The trend in the Commonwealth was for there to be a single industrial trade union with close links to the ruling political party. There was widespread rejection of the ICFTU because of its close links with the former colonial powers.

The PSI Africa conference took place from 25–28 May 1965 in Nairobi, Kenya. Since the outbreak of the Mau-Mau rebellion led by Jomo Kenyatta against the colonial power, Britain, the Kenyan African National Union government had been authoritarian but pro-Western. Behind the scenes at the conference it became clear that even the delegates in attendance rejected paternalistic 'appointees' whose polices had not been coordinated with the local organisations.

The African organisations that had an operational structure also sought independent administration of the PSI aid. 'Africa for the Africans' was the slogan of a movement covering all of black Africa. The PSI Executive reacted by convening an Africa Advisory Committee in the years when there was no regional conference and stepped up its trade union training in the region. The following year, PSI had 155,100 members in Africa, concentrated in the former British colonies of Aden (Forces and Associated Organisations Local Employees Union), Kenya (National Union of Public Service Workers), Mauritius (Federation of Civil Service Unions), Nigeria (Union of Local Authority Staff), Northern Rhodesia (Municipal Workers Union), Zambia (National Union of Local Authorities Workers) as well as in the Alliance des Prolétaires Indépendants du Congo (Alliance of Congo Independent Proletarians) and the Fédération Générale des Fonctionnaires et Ouvriers de l'État (General Federation of Civil Servants and State Workers) in the former French protectorate of Tunisia (the only country with a tradition of trade unions).

The main purpose of the Africa conference was to improve the tense relationship between organisations of public service employees and governments, which was clearly visible at the conference: pro-Western but authoritarian regimes like Hastings Kamuzu Banda's Malawi or Kenneth

Kaunda's Zambia prevented delegates from leaving the country or only allowed them to attend as observers.

The racist regimes in the south caused particular concern: officials of the Northern Rhodesia African Municipal Workers Union were subject to arbitrary arrest; the police monitored meetings; arbitrary mass indictments and convictions made Africa a difficult terrain for part of everyday life. After the white Southern Rhodesian minority government had made its Unilateral Declaration of Independence (UDI), the British cabinet declared the regime illegal and supporting of treason, which caused serious conflicts of loyalty for African public officials. The apartheid regime in South Africa used the so-called Sabotage Act to punish trade unionists, including the death penalty. PSI bodies protested constantly at all imaginable levels – prime ministers, ministers of justice, participants at Commonwealth conferences – and they paid for lawyers and posted bail.

This impacted on PSI, because not only did the conflicting interests of the USA and the USSR directly meet here, but the People's Republic of China also levelled claims of hegemonic behaviour against the other two superpowers. A regional offshoot of the Socialist International – the Asian Socialist Conference – had already foundered on these conflicts, so there was little expectation of support from social democratic parties.

In Kuala Lumpur, Malaysia, where the first conference in this PSI region took place in 1965 at the invitation of the Congress of Unions of Employees in the Public and Civil Services, the president of the host organisation urged in his opening address that delegates 'limit their contributions to trade union matters and waste no time on politics'. Indeed, the only reference made to Vietnam during the conference was in connection with an absent delegate from that country. During discussion of trade union issues, only the delegate from the Israeli Union of Public Service, Clerical and Admin-istrative Employees was able to point proudly to 'his' union's unrestricted right to organise and strike.

Japan, Kuwait and the Philippines had ratified ILO Convention No. 87 and generally complied with it. Burma, Pakistan and Syria had signed on paper but did not comply. The host country, Malaysia, refused to sign Convention No. 87: the country was therefore described by a delegate from the host organisation as democratic in form but not in substance.

As had previously happened at the Nairobi conference, again in Kuala Lumpur the relationship between public service unions and governments was on the agenda. This was no easy issue. PSI and ILO had only just convinced the Japanese government to ratify ILO Convention No. 87, when a request came from the 600,000-strong JICHIRO for support because the Ministry of Education was refusing to negotiate with the teaching union and because trade union activities were attracting disciplinary sanctions. In the Philippines, trade unions had to register. If authorisation was refused on arbitrary grounds, the organisation was illegal and any further activity was punishable under criminal law. The Ceylon Government Clerical Service Union was not allowed to cooperate with unions from other sectors.

Yet this hardship bore fruit. At the beginning of the campaign, PSI had only 17,905 members in the region, but by 1966, 292,702 were organised (although of that number, 50,520 were in India, 34,120 in Malaysia, 25,000 in Singapore and 93,500 in Turkey). This by no means exhausted the full potential. The delegate from the Association of Public Service Unions, from Maharashtra, India, referred to the existing 13,000 registered unions just in India, each of which represented about 5,000 public service workers.

The three regional conferences differed in their economic concepts: the Western Hemisphere Conference of Public Servants in Mexico was silent on issues of economic policy. Asian trade unionists were told that they should increase productivity to a maximum and avoid anything that could put a brake on growth. Africans were called upon to fight for economic independence after obtaining their political independence from their erstwhile colonial masters. As part of any development programme, the monocultural model from the colonial period had to be put aside and land reform carried out. These countries had to build robust infrastructure. Cooperatives were seen as occupying key positions in the future economy. Trade unions had the role of ensuring fair pay and preventing the abuse of international aid to exploit or bully people economically. The centrepiece of this design for Africa was rapidly increasing aid from the developed world – even if it meant a smaller increase in living standards at home. In a speech, PSI President Adolph Kummernuss called this 'a politically astute imperative' because 'a dangerous increase in tension between rich and poor can in no way benefit our world and social system'.

When the three regional members of the Executive from Latin America, Africa and Asia – their appointment had been decided at the 1964 congress – attended meetings in Europe, the overall objective of their joint effort was made crystal clear to them: '*Only those who live in affluence live well*' (Bertolt Brecht). Full employment had become a reality with an average unemployment rate of 1.5 per cent. The pay restraint practised in the difficult post-war years to promote reconstruction appeared to be paying off. Dreams of more radical changes in society were now no more than yesterday's news. There was now a need to adapt old theory to new conditions.

PSI had begun this process of adaptation as early as its conference in 1946. At that meeting, delegates had replaced the clear call for the right to strike that had been contained in their pre-war programmes with a woolly phrase, 'unrestricted right to organise for all employees in public services and public utility works', and there was a simultaneous push for the introduction of 'arbitration services on the basis of parity for the settlement of all conflicts arising from the relations between employers and employees according to the Anglo-American model' (because of massive non-compliance with the law in the Third World). However, the XVI[th] PSI Congress in 1961, held in the Kurhaus in Bad Cannstatt near Stuttgart, called unambiguously for the right to strike.

When it became clear that there was no place in the emerging government-protected entrepreneurial economy for the demands made in Zurich in 1946 for the 'socialisation of all industries and undertakings, the control and management of which is in the general interest of people', the congress in 1958 renounced this goal. Helped by a thaw in international relations (Nikita Khrushchev, made his 'change of direction' speech at the XX[th] Communist Party Conference) in the 1960s, the extension of the welfare state in industrialised countries became the main objective of trade union activity.

Hopes were placed in the Nordic countries, particularly Sweden, where in the post-war years the 'people's home' (*folkhemmet*), or welfare state, had been consistently extended using the ideas of two economists, Gösta Rehn and Rudolf Meidner, who were close to the trade union federation.

From 1960 to 1965, gross national product (GNP) grew on average 5.3 per cent and productivity 5.6 per cent annually while unemployment remained under 2 per cent. Central government and local authorities therefore had sufficient money for all-embracing public administration and comprehensive social provisions, such as democratising education, improving the standard of living of large families and pensioners, equality for the disabled, and generous interventions in the labour market.

The Scandinavian social democrats planned a further restructuring of their welfare states, to introduce equality; yet military and economic crises loomed on the international horizon. The recession of 1964–65 started a long, downward economic trend throughout Europe. Simultaneously, there was a split in the Western alliance as a result of Washington's overwhelming military (and hence political) power and the burgeoning budget deficit in the USA. As a result, the dollar exchange rate declined steadily – because of the controls exerted by the world currency system that was the cornerstone of the *Pax Americana*.* The Gold Standard was wound up in 1968, which spelt the *de facto* end of the convertibility of the dollar. The moment had come for the Euro-dollar, the first truly transnational currency, followed by a gradual removal of all restrictions on movement of capital.

The driving force of the world economy gradually moved to the European and Japanese national economies. Here PSI was in an excellent position from the outset within the European Economic Community (EEC), which had been set up as an alternative to the American integration plan for Europe. PSI had been invited by the ICFTU to represent the organisation at the meetings on European integration that culminated in the signing of the Treaty of Rome in 1957, establishing the EEC.

On the occasion of the tenth jubilee of this event, the Federation of Unions of European Officials called for 'action in the social sphere' that 'at least equals activity in the economic and technical spheres'. The first PSI European conference in 1969 finally called for a joint action programme with other member organisations in the six member states

---

* The long period of growth and 'stability' underpinned by US military and economic power.

of the EEC. Moreover, a resolution referred to the human, social and political consequences of continuous modernisation and established a standing working party on automation.

# 5

# The Crisis Returns

The recession in Europe and the crisis in the USA coincided with the Third World revolutionary wave that for the first time truly melded the stored up frustration in all continents into a movement. '*Power to the people!*' (John Lennon) mobilised not just students in Europe and the USA, but broad groups of those in work, including unionised public service workers.

In Germany, the Gewerkschaft Öffentliche Dienste, Transport und Verkehr (ÖTV) (Union for Public Services and Transport) demonstrated in May 1968 in support of parity co-determination in all large companies and against the emergency legislation of the then coalition CDU/CSU–SPD (Christian Democratic Union/Christian Socialist Union and Social-Democratic Party) government. In Britain, the National Union of General and Public Employees (together with the National Union of Public Employees and the Transport and General Workers Union) called in September 1969 for a pay increase of between 20 per cent and 30 per cent for 770,000 public sector workers. After the Labour government broke off negotiations, strikes spread in spite of a threat to bring in the army. The London refuse collectors obtained an increase in basic pay from £15 9s to £20 which was the decisive breakthrough for a general wage increase of 15 per cent for all council workers, with a knock-on effect for 260,000 hospital auxiliaries, the miners, and postal, electricity and railway workers.

In the wake of the student unrest in Paris in May 1968, the public sector workers in the Fédération des Personnels des Services Publics et des Services de Santé (Federation of Public Service and Health Service Personnel) took part in the general strike. The Federazione Lavoratori Aziende Elettriche Italiane was recognised by the state electricity company as its negotiating partner after a 72-hour nationwide protest action in mid-May. The Unione Italiana Lavoratori Servizi Pubblici (Union of Italian Public Service Workers), that had tenuous links to PSI, took part in both the regional general strike for housing reform in the autumn of 1969 and in the ensuing 1970 nationwide uprising for '*casa, fisco, salute*' ('housing, tax, health').

Although strikes in the public sector were illegal in most federal states in the USA, there was a sharp increase in disputes, from about 15 in 1958 to 254 in 1969. The trade unions were on the offensive. During a dispute involving garbage workers in Memphis, Tennessee, that started because two black employees had been crushed in a transport vehicle and because during bad weather black sanitation workers – but not white – were sent home without pay, the PSI affiliate AFSCME obtained the support of the civil rights movement. Martin Luther King Jr, organiser of the Montgomery bus boycott and of the legendary march on Washington, came to Memphis and declared his support for the strikers, who were under constant attack from the police and 4,000 men of the National Guard with night-sticks, tear gas and live bullets. It was on this occasion that the Nobel laureate made his prophetic speech on 3 April 1968: 'I don't know what will happen now. We have got some difficult days ahead. But it really doesn't matter with me now, because I've been to the mountaintop.' The next day a sniper killed the Baptist preacher, who was standing on a balcony at the Lorraine Hotel.

In 1968, Bill Lucy, who became PSI President in 1994, had worked closely with Martin Luther King Jr. In the tumultuous aftermath of Dr King's assassination, Lucy helped maintain the labour–civil rights community coalition that sealed the workers' victory and became the model used throughout the nation. He was the founder of the Coalition of Black Trade Unionists and also played a leadership role in the non-governmental organisations (NGOs) fighting apartheid in South Africa. When Nelson Mandela was freed from prison, his first trip was to the USA where Lucy coordinated his programme.


## Women in PSI

Women's participation was the bell-wether of the increasing social unrest within PSI. This was not the first time, because they had played a similar role in 1945. Straight after the Allied victory, women were visibly more active within PSI: women officials had said that issues pertaining to women working in the public sector should not be dealt with by means of just a brief reference to them. Two central demands were:

- the right to work for women – ending the temporary nature of women's work
- equality at work and in the union – same pay for the same job.

These issues were discussed at the annual conference of the UK Civil Service Clerical Association, in whose ranks female members were already a majority, and in the ranks of the French affiliate. However, the more the conservative forces in society gained the upper hand, the more such activities simply petered out. It was only in the run-up to the 1968 movement that women were again on the march: in Singapore, nurses had gone on strike because of their poor working conditions and had brought the local unions together in an Amalgamated Union of Public Employees. In Britain, a protest march by 10,000 nurses signalled the start for the shop steward movement.*

Also, within unions, issues specific to women had won greater consideration, starting with an 'International Seminar for Women's Issues in the Public Service' with delegates from seven countries that had prompted similar events in all member organisations. Following hard on the heels of the third revolutionary wave, the Executive Committee accepted a proposal from the Gewerkschaft der Öffentlich Bediensteten (the Austrian Public Services Union) that regular international conferences should be held to discuss matters of interest to women. This led in 1970 to a world conference of professional women in Stockholm that brought together delegates from 20 countries. Future Nobel Prize winner Alva Myrdal, who made an impassioned plea for women to play an active role in society, opened the meeting. She said that if all artificial barriers between the sexes were dismantled, the standard of living would increase by 35 per cent in

---

* The movement initiated in the UK through which militants in unions bypassed national union structures, putting workplace activists in direct touch with those in other workplaces, including those working for multinational companies in other countries, as the basis for industrial action.

France and by as much as 40 per cent in Britain. This was controversial talk. The representatives from the USA and Canada reported on the Women's Liberation Front in their countries that called for drastic changes now. On the other hand, some male delegates were rather sceptical about or even opposed to specific positive action for women. For some delegates, even specific training courses for women were considered controversial.

## The Movements of 1968

Overall, PSI rejected or remained aloof from the issues thrown up by the movement of 1968. For example, the trade secretariat did not even participate in the protests of the ICFTU against the takeover by the fascist military junta in Greece, because the Greek public workers' organisation – in contrast to the trade union federation – was intact and fighting the regime in its own way. (However, support was given to the fighting fund of the underground Spanish trade unions.)

The minutes of the Executive meeting held in The Hague on 21–22 August 1968 contain a staunch protest resolution against the Russian invasion of Czechoslovakia, but no discussion of events in Western Europe. On Vietnam, the rallying point of the third revolutionary wave, where there was a small but active organisation of bus workers in Saigon, the second Asian conference certainly passed a resolution that welcomed the end of air raids and de-escalation of the war. They called for a 'fair and lasting peace'. But the most prominent part of the meeting was a presentation by Gunnar Myrdal, an influential Swedish economist, international civil servant and social democratic politician, on the role of public services in developing countries.

'*Give peace a chance*' (John Lennon). The 1973 congress simply repeated the peace resolution from 1958 – an atomic weapon test ban as a first step to comprehensive disarmament (in fact, one year later the superpowers agreed the Threshold Test Ban Treaty, which only banned underground testing of atomic weapons over 150 kilotons, more than ten times the explosive power than the bomb dropped on Hiroshima – tests that in practice hardly ever took place).

## New Leadership and New Location ...

However, within PSI in these unsettled times a change of generation occurred when the headquarters moved from London to Ferney-Voltaire, near Geneva (where many other trade secretariats and the ILO are based) in 1983. This brought an end to a period of heated factionalism within the organisation. Heinz Kluncker was symbolic of the change. After his successful election as President of ÖTV at the age of 39, the public sector had become the pacesetter for pay settlements, leading in 1974 to a pay increase, achieved by strike action, of 11 per cent. Although Kluncker vehemently defended the USA, and PSI under his leadership advocated the return of US delegates to the ILO (they had left because of the predominantly anti-American atmosphere within the organisation), he was instrumental in the closure of the PSI bureau in Washington that had been used by the CIA.

After his election as President in 1973, Kluncker was in a position to welcome new member organisations after the fall of the last dictatorships in Europe: the Greek ADEDY (Anotate Dioikesis Eneson Demision Ypallelon – Federation of Public Employees Unions), the Portuguese Sindicato dos Trabalhadores da Administração Pública (Trade Union of Public Administration Workers) and the Spanish Federación de Trabajadores de la Administración Pública (Federation of Public Administration Workers).

In the teeth of opposition from member organisations in countries with a colonial past, Kluncker pushed through the closure of the Trade Union Council and greater regionalisation of PSI. The objective was for regional conferences to be independent in their decision-making and in selecting areas of activity for their elected bodies.

## ... and New Regions

A PSI Inter-American Committee was thus established in 1978. Two years later, at the invitation of the Federación Nacional de Trabajadores de Institutos Educacionales de Venezuela (National Federation of Workers in

Educational Institutions of Venezuela) in Caracas, it organised a regional conference in connection with a sector seminar. The participants, including representatives from Nicaragua, enthusiastically welcomed the Sandinista revolution as one of the 'most important events of the decade' but not without recalling their commitment to party pluralism, freedom to organise and press freedom.

The African Regional Advisory Committee was set up in Edinburgh in 1977 and in 1979 organised a regional conference in Freetown, Sierra Leone, where, alongside the Municipal and Local Government Employees Union, two further member organisations with a total of 9,000 members were active. More than in other regions, work in this continent depended on political changes (such as Southern Rhodesia becoming independent Zimbabwe) and massive financial support from the developed world: the German Friedrich Ebert Foundation (Friedrich-Ebert-Stiftung), the Dutch Trade Union Foundation (Stichting Ontwikkelingssamenwerking Vakbeweging), the Institution of Professional Civil Servants in Great Britain and the LO-TCO (the Swedish Trade Union Confederation and the Swedish Confederation for Public Employees, the two main Swedish national trade union centres) all contributed financially. The subsidies were spent mainly on training programmes – for example, a three-year course for 60 future officials in Sierra Leone and Kenya. The PSI secretariat also kept a close eye on the struggle of black workers for trade union rights in South Africa and provided as much diplomatic support as it could muster.

The Asian Regional Advisory Committee was set up in December 1977. Just three years later a regional conference was held in Singapore at the invitation of the Public Utilities Staff Union, the Singapore Housing and Development Board Workers Union, the Singapore Urban Redevelopment Authority Workers Union and the Amalgamated Union of Public Employees (AUPE). The active Chairman, G. Kandasamy (AUPE General Secretary), reported at this meeting on the progress already achieved. Just before the congress Kandasamy had even been able to convince JICHIRO, with a million members, to join – and had done so in Japanese. This brought the New Zealand Public Services Association on board. Subsequently, Asia became PSI's fastest growing region.

## Expanding Membership and Expanding Public Services – and the Backlash

In Europe and the USA, the number of public services workers was also growing in the 1970s after a period of rapid expansion following the Second World War and a period of stability from 1950 to 1960. Often supported by social democratic governments, 1968 was to provide a boost to reform and extension of the welfare state, based on a decentralised new partnership between local politicians, users and the public service workers who were becoming radicalised in many countries. At the PSI congress in 1973 in New York, the Swedish economist Rudolf Meidner developed this approach as a vision of a humane, social service society, in which the public sector was funded through indirect taxation and employed 50–60 per cent of the population.

Such visions were a spur to PSI in the small detail of everyday work. Professional seminars for a fast growing membership (1981: 8,009,954, of which 303,535 in Africa, 1,625,845 in Asia, 1,615,030 in America, 4,465,644 in Europe) and in new sectors (for example, air traffic control, the defence industry, the prison service, journalists, librarians and archivists, technical staff, police officers and customs officials) were to push forward the expansion of the welfare state. The problem of unequal pay for women was tackled actively: in San Jose, California, AFSCME called the first national strike for 'equal pay for work of equal value' in 1981. Public service workers in other federal states followed their lead.

A contrary trend grew out of the long economic downturns of 1974–75 and 1980–82 that produced a cycle of economic crises based on the technology of the US-controlled internet and computer chip industry. All OECD countries reported a clear drop in production and mass unemployment (1970: 10 million; 1978: 20 million; 1988: 30 million) that did not decrease during the periods of economic recovery. The external debt of the Third World exploded – which was of particular benefit to its creditors (from 1973 to 1975 the balance of payments deficit of the non-oil-producing developing countries grew from US$9 trillion to US$38 trillion).

This slowly eroded the economic foundation of centre–left politics based on the welfare state (social democracy). The interlude of the golden age was over. Effectively unseen by the public around the world, Argentina,

Chile and Uruguay became a laboratory for monetarism. To create the unfettered movement of capital as espoused by the neoliberal economist Milton Friedman, a kind of 'short sharp shock' policy was applied in Chile that cut 25 per cent from public expenditure and abolished all state subsidies. A commercialised and decentralised health system and Administradoras de Fondos Pensiones (pension funds) were created, for which employers no longer had to pay a contribution, so as to bring down labour costs. The state school system also succumbed to the privatisation frenzy. The PSI Inter-American regional conference noted with concern such developments in this country that had enjoyed the benefits of a social security system for decades.

These fears proved to be well-founded. Around 1980, the ideological right came to power in important countries, forming governments that supported economic laissez-faire, together with dismantling the welfare state: Ronald W. Reagan in the USA, who at the beginning of his presidency ordered the instant dismissal of the air traffic controllers who were only seeking an improvement of their working conditions; Margaret Thatcher in Britain; Brian Mulroney in Canada and David Lange's Labour government in New Zealand set the tone. What they referred to as a 'stability' policy was really an 'austerity' policy involving the redistribution of wealth from the poor to the rich:

- greater workload (flexible working practices, greater use of part time work)
- reduction of non-wage costs and social benefits
- longer working time by extension of (unpaid) overtime
- reduction of protection such as notice of dismissal and the extension and general application of short-term employment
- shedding of older workers, to make companies 'fitter'
- better exploitation of invested capital either by downward pressure on pay, reduction of pay in real terms or indirectly through higher taxation of pay or consumer taxes (higher value added tax or other consumption taxes).

In contrast, there was no cut in the spending on arms: on the contrary, under Reagan, the USA unleashed a new version of the Cold War.

Already by the time of the XXII[nd] PSI Congress in 1981, that was held for the first time in a developing country, Singapore, the General Secretary Carl Franken reported that 'many of our members have been involved in bitter struggles to protect both their members and the public interest' against rigid monetarist policy, although the 'public services unions have reacted with extreme patience and responsibility'. Beforehand, the European regional conference complained in a document about:

- the transfer of certain activities from the public sector for the benefit of private interests
- structural reforms carried out under the pretext of economy and efficiency leading to a large section of the public being deprived of services to which they are entitled.

A 'policy of full employment supported by the public sector whereby all types of public service are maintained and extended for the benefit of all parts of society' remained PSI's objective. To achieve it, an energy policy, a health policy, an environmental action programme and a series of profiles on the role of the public service, as well as issues specific to working women, were put forward. (All these programmes were bundled together as a Worldwide Policy Programme for the Public Service at the World Congress in Caracas in 1985.) In a joint initiative with all other concerned trade secretariats, the ILO was asked to put pay policy, privatisation and the effects of automation in the public sector onto its agenda.

The European regional conference held in 1983 in Barcelona spoke already of a 'cold-blooded dismemberment of the public services and public values'. The meeting pressed for programmes for full employment and public investment for the expansion of social and public services and creation of new jobs. The following regional conference discussed the same demands within a steadily ageing population.

Between 1983 and 1984, Margaret Thatcher declared war not only on the miners but also on public sector workers. The Iron Lady simply banned staff at the Government Communications Headquarters (GCHQ) from joining a trade union, to ensure confidentiality and uninterrupted service. The British public service unions therefore decided with the support of the ICFTU, PSI and the Trades Union Congress (TUC) to fight for the reversal of the decision at four levels: against the government, through political channels, through the courts and through the ILO. Despite a ruling by the appeal court that the government decision was 'invalid and without effect', the Council of Europe and the European Court of Human Rights declared themselves not competent in the matter. Neither did a series of demonstrations on the first and subsequent twelve anniversaries of the trade union ban change the Iron Lady's or Tories' minds, although the Blair government did reverse it on coming to power in 1997.

*'A social market economy is not a market economy, a social constitutional state not a constitutional state, a social conscience not a conscience, social justice not justice and social democracy not democracy'* (Friedrich von Hayek): this neoliberal credo was espoused by Reagan and Thatcher after their victories over their national trade unions. Using the conveyor belts of the International Monetary Fund (IMF) (the central bank of national central banks), the World Bank (the International Bank for Reconstruction and Development, IBRD) and the International Finance Corporation (a group within the World Bank group that grants loans to governments and/or the private sector) and similar institutions, they forced the expropriation of public property in new sectors: the electricity industry, the telecommunications sector, the water industry, transport, road building and management, and the education system.

The health budgets in sub-Saharan Africa and many Latin American countries were cut by 50 per cent in the 1980s. Even countries with an efficient public health service, such as Jamaica and Sri Lanka, changed direction and moved toward privatisation. The mortality rate rose sharply everywhere. Not even 'Black Monday' on 19 October 1987, which had been triggered by 184 banks going into liquidation in the USA and which nearly caused a stock market crash of 1930s proportions, was enough to stop the onslaught of international capital flows in the form of stock market indices that had become completely detached from economic reality. On the contrary, the game went on: state pension systems and health services were now in the sights of profit-hungry investors.

PSI tried to home in on one strategic point to stop this onslaught – the dismantling of trade union rights. The ILO was asked to counter the trend of using enabling legislation to declare public service workers as 'essential' and thereby deprive them of the right to defend themselves, as well as the tendency of governments to reject genuinely independent mediation and conciliation services.

The Swedish PSI member organisations organised a joint symposium in 1988 for PSI with the Postal, Telegraph and Telephone International (PTTI) workers union under the title 'Defend Yourself Against Attacks on Union Rights'. Discussions centred on a survey carried out by PSI. The participants agreed unanimously that they were dealing with an international phenomenon, whose objective was the undermining of democratic structures, living standards and working conditions.

The following year, the 1989 PSI World Congress in Harare, Zimbabwe, passed a resolution about the activity of the IMF, that 'attempts to impose on countries that seek its help and support the introduction of drastic austerity programmes and drastic cuts in public services, in pay and jobs'. As a counter-strategy, PSI recommended that member organisations in the debtor countries should improve the image of the public sector and its role in 'redistributing from the rich to the poor': they should seek direct involvement in the negotiations between the IMF and the government – regardless of whether it was tactically sound to be party to the agreements reached. An Education Workbook was published as an aid to argument, and it was introduced with the words of a former IMF Managing Director that he'd used in his retirement speech: 'We make or break human life every day of the year as probably no other force on earth has ever done in the past or will ever do again.'

The new version of the Cold War, unleashed by the Reagan administration and its Star Wars programme, made 'Peace and Disarmament' topical issues at the congress. The huge amount of money spent on arms 'should be diverted to programmes that sought constructive solutions to humankind's social, economic and environmental problems'. Barely had this resolution been passed when Ronald Reagan was triumphant. His 'Mister Gorbachev, tear down this wall!' had come true. And PSI delegates gave 'their warmest welcome to the signs of a broad pro-democracy movement in eastern

Europe, particularly the policy of Glasnost and Perestroika in the Soviet Union, the successes of Solidarność in Poland, the creation of free trade unions in Hungary, as well as a process of democratisation within the official Hungarian unions'. PSI promised 'support to all who are struggling to promote democratic change and independent unions, including members of the Trade Union International of Public Services'. Here the barriers with the trade secretariats that belonged to the communist-dominated WFTU appeared to be crumbling.

# 6

# A Third World War or Peace?

After the collapse of 'true socialism' that is interpreted as *The End of History* (Francis Fukuyama), the only remaining military superpower, the USA – with or without UN support – set the strategic boundaries of its new empire – through war (Afghanistan, Iraq, Yugoslavia, Somalia) and/or through military bases or use-rights (in Bosnia–Herzegovina, Bulgaria, Djibouti in northeast Africa, Kyrgyzstan, Poland, Romania, Hungary, Uzbekistan). In Eastern Europe, a race between the USA, Japan and the European Union began for the conquest of these newly opened markets. 'Experts' from multinational companies from all imaginable countries in their business suits always gave the same technical advice about the only true route to happiness – privatisation. They often preached to former apparatchiks who had no problem at all with the new nostrum as long as they kept their old privileges. However, they did not know how handicaps such as obsolete technical plants and methods and a lack of infrastructure could be overcome – and even less when the promise of better days to come would be kept, if it ever were.

Already during the upheavals, PSI used the ICFTU to find partners in Central and Eastern Europe because the state and territorial structures were often not clear. In Poland, Heinz Kluncker had already attended the first two Solidarność congresses on behalf of PSI and the ICFTU and held private talks with Lech Wałęsa, the Solidarność President. Building on this trust the Service Employees International Union (USA/Canada) was soon able to run a seminar for the Solidarność health service workers.

These tangible training activities were organised with other (potential) members: for the Českomoravský odborový svaz pracovníků služeb (Czech-Moravian Trade Union of Workers in Services) in the Czechoslovak Federal Republic, PSI developed a training programme covering health and safety, labour law and work organisation – but this left aside issues such as the introduction of a new employment status now that 'all citizens are entrepreneurs who employ nobody'.

Just one year after the fall of Nicolae Ceaușescu, the AFL–CIO donated funds for training of the Romanian health service Sindicatul Sanitas, which taught about trade union organisational structures and membership drives and included special training on infectious diseases such as HIV/AIDS.

PSI offered employees in the Bulgarian public health service a seminar on planning trade union development that mainly covered the urgently needed knowledge on collective agreements, as they had applied in hospitals and clinics since the collapse of the old system. Furthermore, the trade secretariat supported a nationwide strike of medical staff.

In Hungary, where, during the changeover period, several PSI members had been in contact with the previously pro-government Magyar Szak-szervezetek Országos Szövetsége (National Confederation of Hungarian Trade Unions) public sector unions and/or the Democratic League, PSI cooperated with both, until clear structures emerged in the country, with a particular emphasis on privatisation projects.

The Finnish organisation Kunnallisten Työntekijäin ja Viranhaltijain Liitto (Municipal Workers' and Civil Servants' Union) took on the task of contacts with the Baltic States and the USSR, where there was an ex-official union and an alternative union movement, both of which duplicated the other to some extent.

Concerning applicant unions from Central and Eastern Europe, there was no agreement among existing affiliates in the PSI between those who refused to cooperate with former communists and those who were inclined to integrate the former state unions. Most of the conflicts among potential new members and old Western European unions emerged about privatisation and a free market economy, an ideology which initially created some euphoria in the East, that was enhanced by Western think tanks, who tried to influence decisions through major financial incentives.

Dissension within PSI about applications from Central and Eastern Europe arose chiefly from the general euphoria in these societies for privatisation and the market economy. The health service section of Solidarność, which had just escaped the claws of a command economy, was a fervent supporter of the American model. However, after numerous private conversations with officials and experts and reading the PSI education workbook *Privatisation: A Trade Union Response*, the delegates from Estonia, Latvia, Lithuania, the former USSR, the Czech Republic, the Nordic states and Germany, meeting in Vilnius in 1992, passed a resolution which said:

> The Nordic countries have well-developed market systems, now threatened, and the German system of public administration has many admirers. There was also much about public services in Britain that was well worth defending from the ravages of Thatcherism. Less attractive examples are the absence of a national health service in the United States and the way in which public services in Latin America are being systematically destroyed by structural adjustment.

In 1992, the European regional conference was held in Prague in conjunction with the general assembly of the European Public Services Committee and this led to the creation of a European Federation of Public Service Unions (EPSU). The PSI's expansion into Eastern Europe, that had begun with the accession of the first member organisations at an Executive Board meeting on 13–14 November 1991, was advanced by the setting up of three coordination units in Prague, Bucharest and Kiev (later to become sub-regional secretariats) and by sending a fact-finding mission to Moscow, and subsequently led to new members from Georgia and Azerbaijan, following membership from unions in the Czech Republic, Hungary, Estonia, Romania and Bulgaria.

The effects of economic instability on women, particularly in this region, was therefore one of the subjects for discussion at the World Women's Conference held in Singapore in 1992, which met under the motto 'Women and Development' and 'Women and Power' (on which subject Nancy Riche from the National Union of Public and General Employees gave a spirited keynote address).

The XXV[th] World Congress in 1993, held in Helsinki, Finland, was attended by 637 delegates and 74 observers, who represented 265 member organisations from 97 countries with a total membership of 16 million members. PSI had finally become a global player – an enthralling success, which, of course, brought new challenges.

The constitution, which provided for four advisory regional committees (Africa, Asia–Pacific, Europe and the Inter-Americas), needed updating. Simultaneously, priorities in terms of structure and policy content had to be changed. PSI headquarters should act chiefly as an information clearing house, whilst the regional groups were responsible for PSI's overall policy relevant to their work, in which task they were to be supported by sub-regional offices that were as yet to be established.

The enlarged PSI Executive should provide a clearer steer on programming priorities at its annual meeting. Only the Women's Committee and the Public Sector Working Group should be considered 'evergreen'. All other working parties (there were eleven at one stage), such as Equality of Opportunity, Youth, Indigenous Peoples, Migrant Workers, Central and Eastern Europe, should be of limited duration from now on.

Modern technology should be used to boost efficiency. All activities should be centred on action/results, not meetings – and the same applied to the PSI congresses held every four years. This body's vital task should be to make decisions about an action programme drawn up by the member organisations. A PSI publication, *Charting a Union's Future*, called on all members in 1995 to establish their political agenda for the next five years and to develop their plans for organising, membership drives, strengthening links with other unions, and so on. In addition, a common response had to be found to a series of outstanding issues:

- Should PSI now work with the WFTU and its professional groups, dominated by the communists?
- Should PSI create an associate membership for organisations who simply wanted to be on the mailing list?
- What should be the relationship with allied trade secretariats, particularly where the demarcation lines were blurring because of privatisation, outsourcing and public–private partnerships?
- Should PSI concentrate on its shrinking core activity in the public sector or devote itself to the services sector as a whole, both public and private?

- Should PSI help the employees of private service providers to organise?
- If PSI accepted that small, independent unions are bound to fail when attempting to solve international problems because they have no chance against multinational companies, the World Bank and, later, the World Trade Organisation, then are mergers needed?

However, the question then arises of how to bring the organisation's accumulated knowledge and know-how and its members' loyalty unscathed through this restructuring process.

## Neoliberals and the Welfare State

In fact, the neoliberals had failed in their idea that they would revitalise capitalism through redistribution – all they had created was a boom-bust cycle of the kind that had existed before the economic crisis. '*Blowing with the wind of change*'* (The Scorpions), the exponents of finance capital nevertheless stepped up their social offensive. The IMF, the World Bank and the US Treasury jointly produced the Washington Consensus, which governments had to accept if they wanted loans. The ten points of this structural adjustment programme included:

1. strict limits on the budgetary deficit
2. low interest policy
3. reduction of marginal tax rates
4. privatisation of state-owned enterprises
5. deregulation
6. trade liberalisation
7. no barriers to foreign direct investment
8. the reorientation of public expenditures towards areas of high economic returns and redistributive sectors such as health and education
9. managed exchange rates to promote new exports
10. securing property rights.

* A song in which you are asked to picture Moscow and its people – soldiers and citizens – contemplating what might be possible in the transition to capitalism.

It is not a coincidence that at this time efforts failed to make the European Social Charter (the EU's attempt to inject social concerns into the economic project that had been the EU until then) a binding standard, whilst, in contrast, the European Commission passed a public procurement directive (that may not be repealed under national law) for coordination of procedures for awarding public service contracts. It opened the public sector to bidders from all EU states.

It was no coincidence that the Liberal government in Australia – a country with a developed network of collective agreements and a high level of state intervention – neutralised important parts of the right to collective bargaining in the first wave of their conservative reform agenda.

This social trend even affected parts of the social democratic fabric. For the UK's New Labour, for example, the 'lean state' – converting public poverty (also known as indebtedness) into private wealth – was at the top of their political agenda.

Pushed into a corner by its traditional allies, PSI nevertheless tried to resist. A privatisation conference took place in 1991 that reacted to the 'devastation of the public sector' by amending the World Wide Programme for the Public Service that had been agreed at the World Congress in Caracas in 1985. A particularly pressing question was whether PSI should remain wedded to the Keynesian notion of the role of the public sector despite the irreversible changes that had happened very quickly in many countries. The conference decided that PSI would continue to support a strong public sector that offered universal access to a broad range of services, including:

- an economic infrastructure for transport, energy, communications, water supply, sewerage and drainage, housing and other utilities
- a full range of public health services
- educational and vocational training services providing opportunities for all age groups including childcare
- strong institutions for the protection of the natural environment
- provision of internal and external security
- employment and labour market services

- cultural and recreational services, including broadcasting, public parks and national parks
- institutions for international relations and foreign trade
- banking, financial and insurance services
- taxation systems and services.

The objective remained what it always had been, the welfare state. PSI President Monika Wulf-Mathies, elected to succeed Victor Gotbaum in 1989, described its constituent parts as 'action management, modern social and health centres and municipal environmental centres'. Public sector trade unions should stop simply defending past achievements, and cooperate with the workforce to make proposals for an optimum service and cost reduction. Even active involvement in redundancies was no longer a taboo subject. PSI's precondition for this cooperation was genuine social dialogue at all levels.

This principle was subsequently publicised in both policy documents and in agit-prop publications (*The Origins of Privatisation, Public Service and Private Interest, Privatisation in Transitional Economies, International Trade Agreements and Trade Unions*). *In the Public Interest?*, written by Brendan Martin, a former researcher of the British National and Local Government Officers Association, had been commissioned and published by PSI. The president of the Sveriges Kommunaltjänstemannaförbund (Swedish Union of Local Government Officers, SKTF) and PSI executive member Sture Nordh, published a book with the title *Välfärdstatens vägval och villkor* (The Welfare State at a Crossroads). A video entitled *Doing it Publicly* was produced to explain the issues to people who were not public officials.

## Getting the Facts Right

PSI started to make far greater use of computer technology when collating material that could help with their opposition to privatisations. The pioneer in this area had been an initiative of nearly all UK PSI members – the creation of the Public Services Privatisation Research Unit (PSPRU) to help in union opposition to the Iron Lady. This research facility had collected all the important data on privatisation ranging from the profitability of whole economic sectors to the earnings of individual companies, and stored the information on both computer and microfiche so it could be retrieved by trade unions. At the beginning of the 1990s, PSI started to be aware of the need to take care for itself of the development of such databases. In the late 1990s, the PSPRU became the Public Services International Research Unit (PSIRU), based at the University of Greenwich, whose director, David Hall, published *Public Services Work* in 2005 for PSI.

The PSIRU took over the older PSPRU databases and integrated them into a worldwide system that included material on the role of international consultants/auditors such as PriceWaterhouseCoopers in justifying privatisations. The databases that the PSIRU manages for PSI hold material on water, energy, waste, health services and prisons. This has produced a comprehensive system that covers areas such as: the municipal waste management industry in Europe, WMX Technologies/Waste Management International, Nordic countries and deregulated markets, privatisation of electricity and gas in Asia. This, in turn, gave rise to a quarterly PSI Research Network News that was sent to subscribers by email. Feedback produced not only new information for the PSIRU databases but also new contacts with committed union members, experts and journalists.

PSI used new communication systems when dealing with issues such as the World Bank and globalisation: cartoon figures from comic books on both of these issues talked about the IMF and the World Bank (*A Tale of Power, Plunder and Resistance*) or on how to deal with the World Trade Organisation (WTO) and the OECD. PSI showed its flexibility in terms not only of form but also of content. In 1997 (exactly ten years after the first post-war crash), speculation by institutional investors against the Thai baht caused the failure of the Asian financial system, and a complete collapse was only averted by the IMF firefighting with $100 billion.

This caused another serious wobble in the IMF's and World Bank's growth model. A number of NGOs and trade unions (including PSI) were asked by these institutions to be part of the Structural Adjustment Participatory Review Initiative. Despite some misgivings, PSI agreed and has subsequently worked on a number of the Bank's annual World Development Reports and participated in professional development programmes organised by the World Bank department responsible for privatisation of public sector companies.

Finally a former PSI Executive Committee member, John Fryer, a past President of the Canadian National Union of Public and General Employees (NUPGE), was seconded to the World Bank for three months as a representative of the public sector. Although he was completely isolated from the other employees and his work was sabotaged, he felt the exercise had not been a complete failure – after all, he had been able to point to the need for the World Bank to pursue a policy of wide-ranging consultation with public service unions.

## Trade Union Rights

In its opposition to the World Bank, PSI was able to network with NGOs for the first time. Even in the 1980s efforts to cooperate with religious, political or social-ethnic organisations had failed. Amnesty International had been the only exception, as PSI had cooperated closely with it after a series of egregious infringements of human and trade union rights had caught the attention of the non-union public. What follows are some of the rights issues on which PSI has taken action in recent years.

In 1980, Abdullah Basturk, President of both the trade union umbrella organisation DISK (Türkiye Devrimci Isci Sendikalari Konfederasyonu – Confederation of Revolutionary Workers' Unions of Turkey) and the PSI-affiliated Genel Is (Genel Hizmetler İşçileri Sendikası – Public Service Employees Union), along with 1,477 fellow trade unionists, had been brought before a judge after a military coup in Turkey, and President Heinz Kluncker; the chairman of Kommunal, Sigvard Marjasin, and General Secretary Hans Engelberts travelled to the country several times to make prison visits, accepting interrogations lasting days and surveillance by the secret police. (PSI translated Basturk's defence speech into English and published it as a book.)

In 1982, the president of the new Chilean affiliate Asociación Nacional de Empleados Fiscales (National Association of Fiscal Employees), Tucapel

Jiménez, was killed in cold blood. (PSI protested strongly to the Chilean government.)

In 1986, the PSI Assistant General Secretary, Harry Batchelor, addressed a demonstration of 157 members of the Black Health and Allied Workers Union of South Africa who had been dismissed. Subsequently, Moses Mayekiso, with his brother and three others, was charged in June 1986 with high treason, sedition and endangering the state. (The coordinated intervention of Amnesty International and PSI that called upon member organisations to campaign for a withdrawal of pension fund investments in South Africa brought about their acquittal by a court in 1989.)

In 1988, Manuel Bustos and Arturo Martines, President and Vice President of the Comando Nacional de Trabajadores (National Workers Commando) in Chile, were sentenced to 541 days' detention for 'endangering national security' and international protests, including PSI's, forced the sentence to be changed to 'internal exile'.

After the Asian financial crisis in 1997, the Korean regime under President Kim Dae Jung – allegedly obeying instructions of the IMF – imprisoned 209 trade unionists in one year. (Hans Engelberts took part in demonstrations held in the subsequent years that were attacked by the police, visited activists in prison, organised worldwide protests and negotiated with five different Korean Ministers of Labour on changing the country's labour law. After multiple protests by PSI and several NGOs, the founding congress of the Korean Government Employees Union was due to take place on 23 March 2001. However, just before it began, eight squadrons of rapid-response police stormed the auditorium at the Korea University and arrested 178 participants. The repression did not end there. Here are a few examples among many: on 20 October 2003, the riot police arrested hundreds who were attending a Korean Government Employees Union (KGEU) rally in Seoul; in 2004, President Young Gil Kim and General Secretary Byeong Soon Ahn were arrested, and a further 17 KGEU members were arrested, 1,143 trade unionists were dismissed, 342 had their pay cut by two thirds, and 76 received an official reprimand.)

In 2002 alone in Colombia, 180 trade unionists were murdered by paramilitary groups which cooperated with the army. PSI, in cooperation with the member organisation Sindicato de Trabajadores de EMSIRVA

(Trade Union of EMSIRVA Workers), launched a campaign on International Human Rights Day that included a letter writing campaign to the government and several state institutions and an international mission. In 2005, the ILO sent observers to the country to investigate the countless complaints about infringement of the right to organise and, in 2006, the Colombian government finally approved a permanent ILO mission to the country.

## New Work with NGOs ...

As a result of enhanced cooperation in the 1990s between PSI and the increasing number of NGOs (these were now keen on seeking solutions by consensus), a kind of cross-fertilisation took place. For example, PSI organised a conference about the environment (this would once have been an irritant to some trade unionists) that led to the creation of an environmental action programme. The International now paid more attention to its women members within its various bodies and strived for gender-neutral language at its meetings; a women's positive action plan was produced.

The traditional PSI, which had been fixated on infringement of trade union rights, now opened up not only to the issues faced by migrant workers in cooperation with the International Migrants Right Watch Committee but also to the concerns of gays and lesbians at work; it organised a conference on the issue and worked with the ILO to produce a brochure on HIV and AIDS. In contrast, the NGOs' campaign against the Multilateral Agreement on Investment (MAI) was well-advanced before PSI's affiliates fully understood the coup that trade ministers were attempting to commit in the interests of multinational companies.

## ... On Water, For Example

The new architecture of PSI was shown at its most striking in the growing importance of strategic campaigns. A case in point is water – a vital part of our daily needs and the global environment. Around 40 per cent of the world's population suffers acute water shortages. More polluters and poor maintenance of the mains supply systems (in industrialised countries), drought and the ensuing soil erosion and the lack of both financial and technical resources to build a mains water system (in developing countries) are critical problems. The water supply system is the most important of all infrastructure services because of its direct impact on health. Also, early experience with water companies like Compagnie Générale des Eaux, France, and Thames Water, England, illustrated that 'privatisation equals price increase'.

PSI therefore vehemently advocated in its own water programme, that water supply – privatised or not – must always carry the hallmarks of a publicly owned utility. This meant that whenever private companies – by which PSI meant multinationals – were involved in any way in the water supply business, there had to be effective and guaranteed public control and accountability. This was the aim of an International Code of Conduct for Water Supply drawn up at the PSI water conference in Stockholm in August 1995.

Simultaneously, the WHO made 'clean water' a cornerstone of its campaign 'Health for All by 2000'. At the International Conference on Freshwater sponsored by the German government and held in December 2002, and which brought together ten PSI member organisations, the World Bank, a great many UN agencies and delegates from 120 governments, trade unions were for the first time given a formal role in decisions about the restructuring of public water supply systems. Various attempts to 'liberalise' the European 'water market' had failed due to vigorous resistance from bodies such as the Bundesverband der Deutschen Gas- und Wasserwirtschaft (German Federation of the Gas and Water Industry). The Swiss government was forced to put the issue to the Swiss people in a referendum. In response, the multinational companies and the European Commission, as part of the WTO's General Agreement on Trade in Sevices (GATS) negotiations, insisted that a total of 72 developing countries open their markets.

Resistance grew, and PSI was part of it. A few examples:

- Using the PSIRU databases, the Philippine General Santos City Government Employees Association, with the support of NGOs, began a fierce campaign against the privatisation of the Metropolitan Water Supply by the Sewage Company of Manila.
- Conferences in Venezuela and Honduras considered the creation of a regional network of water workers. PSI commissioned a survey of privatisations in Argentina, Bolivia, Brazil, Chile, Colombia, Ecuador and Peru, linked to similar initiatives in Europe, Inter-America and North America.
- PSI, with the South African Municipal Workers Union (SAMWU) and the Confederation of South African Trade Unions, started a campaign against Biwater (a multinational water company) privatisation plans in South Africa.
- At a PSI world conference on public utilities at which delegates exchanged experiences, David Hall, director of the PSIRU, released a survey that attracted a lot of news media attention about the water industry's profit margins. He later presented his findings at the congress of the Canadian Union of Public Employees (CUPE), which saw the start of another regional campaign for public investment in the water supply.
- SAMWU highlighted the corruption that had arisen from the privatisation of the Lesotho Highlands Water Project.
- PSI, with NGOs, successfully intervened in the World Water Forum held on 17–22 March 2000 in The Hague, an event sponsored by the World Bank and multinational companies.
- At the next World Water Forum in Kyoto from 6–23 March 2003, PSI and the Japanese Trade Union Centre, RENGO, organised a workshop that produced a union declaration drawing heavily on the PSIRU publication *Water in Public Hands*. The multinationals were becoming less interested in the water sector in developing countries, as they were unable to convince investors seeking quick profits to make the necessary long-term investment.
- This campaign was of course taken up by the rank and file at the World Social Forum in Mumbai, India, and at the PSI Women's Committee's workshop, 'Las Mujeres y la defensa del agua como un

derecho humano' ('Women and the defence of water as a human right') in Peru.

- During the World Water Forum 4 in Mexico City on 16–22 March 2006, organised by the World Water Council, four members of the PSI delegation were refused visas by the conservative Mexican government, which considered them potential troublemakers. However, even such repressive measures could not prevent the sustainable success of the campaign.

The campaign has been successful: despite all the efforts of the multinationals, so far only 5 per cent of all water services are in private hands. More importantly, PSI was becoming a campaigning organisation.


## Globalisation

At the start of the new millennium, PSI repositioned itself through its consistent commitment to globalisation issues. Member organisations had accepted that the public services must involve and engage sections of the population – users and NGOs – in planning and evaluating services. Moreover, PSI had joined a movement with a fresh perception of international solidarity that was both controlled by and carried out by working people of all kinds at plant, grassroots and community level.

The International did not act alone in opposition to the flat refusal of the WTO, at its meeting in Seattle, to include a link between trade and labour standards in the texts of its agreements/treaties. Instead, it brought together NGOs and a group of trade unions to discuss how they could act effectively in unison. The most striking result of this rapprochement was PSI's joining two coalitions of NGOs: Our World Is Not For Sale (OWINFS) and Stop the GATS Attack!

PSI was therefore directly involved in coalition planning for the action on the ground against the WTO ministerial conferences in Doha, Qatar (2001), Cancún, Mexico (2003) and in Hong Kong (2005). This cooperation with these new groups and forms of internationalism has crystallised around the World Social Forums.

Even allies that had been thought lost from the ranks of the social democrats moved closer: the European Socialists held a conference 'Social Democracy in a Globalised World' in Copenhagen on 10 October 2002. After suffering electoral defeat in several countries, the delegates at the conference grasped that the root causes of the burgeoning crisis – the mistreatment of millions through mass unemployment, increasing poverty and dwindling prospects for the young – were slowly returning society to the 1930s. Hans Engelberts therefore called on this occasion for a genuinely progressive alliance. He maintained that it could not be right that British Labour Party Congresses vote overwhelmingly against private finance initiatives only for Tony Blair to say that he will ignore the vote.

## The First Steps of the New Century

The temporary keystone of PSI's new architecture that had developed after the collapse of 'true existing socialism' was put in place by the delegates at the World Congress in Ottawa from 2–6 September 2002 in the form of an action programme. With Ylva Thörn, Kommunal, Sweden, as its new President, PSI set out to change the direction of globalisation. The core components following from Ottawa have been as follows:

- A 'Pay Equity Now!' campaign run by the PSI Women's Committee, which involved publication not just of a brochure with practical advice on how to achieve equal pay for equal work between men and women, but also of a CD and a regular newsletter.
- The new PSI constitution laid down an obligatory 50:50 gender rule for all of its constitutional bodies and conferences.
- With the slogan 'Giving Young Workers a Voice in Trade Unions', the International tried to encourage its members to adopt inclusive young workers' policies. On the basis of the European Youth Charter, a European young workers' network was created which addressed all workers under the age of 35.
- Through the Millennium Development Goals, the UN and governments from around the world had promised to remove the

gap between rich and poor by 2015, despite the fact that 'prospects of getting money from the centre ... for the countries on the periphery are vanishing'. PSI, in its congress-mandated Quality Public Services Campaign, called this promise to mind under the motto 'Everybody Deserves High-Quality Public Services to Improve their Lives'.

- PSI subsequently joined a global mobilisation advocating high-quality public services as a means to tackle poverty (the Global Call to Action against Poverty). This campaign, which had the support of Nelson Mandela, and a white bracelet as its symbol, started with an appeal at the World Social Forum in 2005 and continued at a series of events for World Women's Day, campaigns for trade and education, as well as demonstrations and appearances at the 2005 G8 Summit, the UN Summit of Heads of State and Government and the Hong Kong WTO Ministerial Conference.

- PSI actively participated in the work of the ILO World Commission on the Social Dimension of Globalisation and as an active stakeholder at the United Nations Conference on Trade and Development (UNCTAD), at the UN Commission on the Status of Women and, via the Trade Union Advisory Committee (TUAC), in the Public Management Committee of the OECD.

More specifically, as part of a campaign that was being developed as this history was being written, PSI has joined a coalition to work on a General Agreement on Public Services (GAPS). The GAPS campaign wants to close the following gaps:

- *the resources gap:* between the services people need and the capacity for providing them
- *the accountability gap:* between those who make decisions and those whose lives depend on them
- *the equity gap:* between services available to the poor and those available to the better-off
- *the gender gap:* between the burden on women of failing services and their involvement in how they are run

- *the labour gap:* between actual and required investment in a workforce whose rights and knowledge are respected
- *the ethical gap:* between the values required in public services and corruption by state abuse and the profit motive
- *the performance gap:* between inadequate systems and equipment and the potential of democratic reform
- *the sustainability gap:* between the need for effective water, energy and transport services and protection of the environment.

Those from PSI ranks who are fighting poverty are convinced that the Millennium Development Goals could be reached on time. Campaigns on the goals of a millennium seem an appropriate activity at which to finish a centennial history of Public Services International as it embraces the twenty-first century '*We shall overcome!*'*

And so, 100 years after the foundation of what had started as basically an international union for public utility workers, where are things now, under the leadership of PSI President Ylva Thörn, President of Swedish affiliate Kommunal? Public utility workers have become a minority – albeit a very activist minority – sector within a general public sector international. What was a male-dominated global union federation is now very much a female-dominated body, organising workers across all sections of a wide public sector – not just a public services – movement. That does not mean that women have 'won' – there are still swathes of the public sector union movement where gender equity is still a major challenge.

President Ylva Thörn's own union has been very active in continuing the century-old struggle to ensure that public utilities – municipal or national – remain public; her union has been at the forefront of winning wage equity for low-paid women workers. She personally has been active in participating in PSI missions to troubled parts of the world where public sector workers and their unions face oppression and organising challenges that workers in the North had assumed were confined to history. Ylva has been central to ensuring that the PSI quality public services campaign is

* This was originally an African-American gospel song, which employees of the American Tobacco Company sang on the picket line in 1946. It is nowadays known as hymn of the civil rights movement.

not just a slogan but is central to organising public sector workers to win their own rights, and also to be allies with the users of public services in developing services that will be the basis of sustainable development and the achievement of the Millennium Development Goals.

Has PSI achieved the objectives set by its founding European fathers? By no means. Has it laid the foundation for public sector unions across the world to complete this task? For sure.

# Part Two

## The History of Public Services: Public Services Have Made Life and the World Better

# Introduction

Throughout human history, cooperation has brought more success and has done so more reliably than single-handed efforts. The rise of great civilisations is inseparable from communal human activity and increasing division of labour. Among the first public services were institutions that watched over public order and security. Buildings were erected to celebrate state religions, and tax authorities raised the funds needed for such public undertakings. The main purpose of these early services was to bolster the power of the ruling elites. Services to improve the lives of ordinary people, such as organised water supply, were the exception rather than the rule.

It was the modern development of more democratic societies that gave rise to such services aimed at the public good. Many of these services evolved as a result of the rapid growth of urban communities in the nineteenth century. As these communities grew into big cities, privately organised water supply, sewerage and solid waste disposal systems failed, as did privately owned energy utilities and transport companies. The result was a boom of newly founded communal systems in the late nineteenth century.

The wave of communalisation immediately led to more effective controls, improved the provision of services to the public and helped create better workplace conditions. The principle of public service provision was so successful that it was adopted very quickly in developed cities, especially in Europe, and remained in place throughout the twentieth century, notwithstanding massive political and historical changes. In the post-war era in particular, public service provision contributed substantially to unprecedented economic growth and wealth creation.

Public spending on hospitals and extensive healthcare systems that provided affordable medical services resulted in greatly improved public health, with a marked decline in infant mortality and gain in longevity. Public water supply and waste disposal systems were crucial in preventing diseases and epidemics. In the industrialised world, wider access to education triggered a genuine 'education explosion', and social services were important in stabilising the incomes of major sectors of the population. Childcare facilities enabled countless women to take on paid employment. Public services decisively improved the lives of women, contributing to gender equality. For the first time, millions of elderly people benefited from pensions and social and health services to support them in their old age. Public energy utilities ensured the reliable provision of affordable energy to the recovering economies after the Second World War.

In the 1950s and 1960s, many countries enjoyed strong economic growth. There was general agreement on the benefits of full employment, which was defined as a policy objective, not just by trade unions but also by governments and industry. Looking back, it is easy to see that period almost as a 'golden age'.

The first voices to speak out against the role of public services and throw doubt on their successes were raised in the 1980s. The backlash occurred not only in response to trade unions' calls for greater shares in corporate profits and for more participation in companies' decision-making processes, but also as a reaction to the rebirth of the feminist movement, the emergence of green politics, the rebellion of the South against the rich North, and because of the prospect of the rising costs of the social systems.

Because we also saw a deceleration of growth, Keynesian policies were discarded, as was the consensus on public tasks. The public sector's role as a promoter of collective social responsibility was upstaged by the new monetarist conception of the public sector as something inherently undesirable and economically inefficient. Trade unions, the state and public services were portrayed as obsolete. What followed were cutbacks in public services and public spending. It was easy to cast the government and its bureaucracy as enemies, given that everyone may at some point have some unfavourable experience in dealing with public authorities. The World Bank and the International Monetary Fund were the first to step into the ring, forcing the privatisation of public services. Margaret Thatcher followed. Public services were handed over en masse to the private sector, and unions were decimated, with the loss of millions of unionised jobs. In the 1990s, the communist ideology with its public sectors was replaced by another ideology: to quote Hans Engelberts, General Secretary of PSI from

1981 to date (his tenure is due to end in September 2007), the 'tyranny of unrestrained market forces unaccountable to the people'.*

We now have a wealth of historical experience of privatisation policy. And we all see that there is a huge difference between the theoretical concept of a market economy and the reality facing people, employers and trade unions. The past decades are full of examples of how the private sector market forces alone fail to secure efficiency and equity. As a rule, privatisation has not only failed to improve the quality of health services, it has also made them more expensive and reduced the number of people who have access to these services. The liberalisation of the sector has drawn health workers away from where they are needed, and has clearly reduced the chances of less developed countries to build modern health systems. Life expectancy is declining in many areas, and as social and other public services are reduced, women are being pushed out of the labour market and back into their traditional roles as homemakers and mothers. Where provisions for old age are concerned, privatisation has exposed pension systems to the enormous risks of the stock markets, causing substantial cost to governments and the insured at the same time. Wherever water supply systems were privatised, the effects were detrimental to consumers, and neither has the privatisation of energy supply utilities yet yielded any public benefit. Private security services are a growth sector, resulting in an unequal distribution of security. As the quality of the privatised services declines, costs and fees increase. The services no longer cover the entire territory of a nation state. Workers lose material benefits and working conditions deteriorate. Those who can afford private services are still being served and they are the only ones who count – for the private companies.

This 'war on government' waged in the name of neoliberal ideology is among the main reasons for the deterioration of many people's living conditions and the aggravation of a series of global problems. Neoliberalism's generous promises of wealth for all have remained unfulfilled. More than 1 billion people live in abject poverty today and one quarter of the world's population have no access to clean drinking water. More than 800 million are unemployed or underemployed, and the gap between rich and

* Hans Engelberts' opening speech at a PSI privatisation seminar in Vilnius, Lithuania, 10–12 March 1992.

poor keeps widening. The consequences are civil unrest, political upheavals, racism, crime, war and terrorism.

Economic globalisation has not been accompanied by global social responsibility for human life. Focusing on short-term profit at the expense of long-term development, neoliberalism has caused and will continue to cause enormous economic and social damage, benefiting only the tiny elites. There is a stark contrast between the few who have grown rich through privatisation and the millions who have lost the jobs on which they depended for their livelihood.

Naturally, public services are not always blameless, perfect and free from corruption. But as Mike Waghorne from PSI said, 'if your sink leaks or your paint is peeling, you don't burn down or sell the house – you fix the sink and repaint'.*

The world is richer today than it ever was. Deficiencies in communal services are often the result of a wilfully provoked lack of funding. The more a government leans towards antisocial, authoritarian policies, the more it will spend on a repressive state machinery to defend itself against popular anger, and the less money will be used for public services to improve people's lives.

Global solidarity and cooperation are critical for the survival of human communities. It remains a challenge throughout the world, especially in the developing countries and for the trade unions, to ensure universal access to public services for all people. This includes public responsibility for such services in order to guarantee solidarity for all.

There are many reasons why public services will be even more urgently needed in the future, including global population growth, the increasing scarcity of jobs, the growing danger of further impoverishment in many regions, and the continued reckless exploitation of natural resources. Public services are needed to ensure adequate protection of human health, to provide job opportunities, sufficient incomes, well-being and protection against life's misfortunes. Public services have contributed substantially to the well being of humanity. They must, can and will continue to do so in the future – because this is what the people want and what the trade unions are fighting for.

* Quoted by Susan George in her preface 'Fixing the Sink and Repainting the House', *Public Services Yearbook 2005/6*.

# 7

# Health Services

## Historical Development

In antiquity, people used home remedies and private healers when they were ill. Traditionally, treating the sick was also a function of religious institutions and their healing cults. In ancient Egypt, for example, the temples also served as places of treatment for the sick. In the second millennium BC, ancient Egypt introduced the first system of publicly provided healthcare with healers paid by the community. The beginnings of medicine as a rational science based on the study of nature date back to the fifth century BC and are associated with Hippocrates, the Greek father of medicine. The first centre of medical training was founded in Alexandria. The earliest known records of independent healthcare institutions are from Sri Lanka (fourth century BC) and India (third century BC), while the first training hospitals for medical experts were established in Persia. The Romans founded hospitals in the first century BC, mainly for the treatment of soldiers and gladiators.

Christianity promoted caring for the sick, and most medieval hospitals were run by monks or nuns and also served as poorhouses and lodgings for pilgrims. Several outstanding medical centres developed in the Arab world in the eleventh and twelfth centuries. The eighteenth century saw the establishment of the first 'modern' hospitals. The Charité hospital in Berlin was founded in 1710 to care for victims of the bubonic plague, and other big cities soon also established large hospitals (Philadelphia 1713, London 1724, Vienna 1784). Their function gradually changed from the provision of healthcare services to the poor to that of modern diagnostic and treatment facilities which also began to train physicians and nursing staff.

In the nineteenth and twentieth centuries, industrialisation and the misery of the working masses in developing countries turned health policy into a central concern of governments. The so-called social question became an ever more explosive issue. In continental Europe, new hospitals were generally built and run with public funding.

Today, health services operate worldwide, albeit at very different levels of quality. While sophisticated, state-of-the-art medical services are available to inhabitants of the world's big cities, there are still large regions that lack even basic healthcare. While medicine helps to continuously increase longevity in the most developed countries, millions of people still suffer and are killed by avoidable diseases every year in other parts of the world because they have no access to medical treatment. In hardly any other field is the global inequality of distribution more marked than where human health and life expectancy are concerned.

## Europe

Fearing revolutionary inclinations among workers in Germany, in 1889 Emperor Wilhelm I approved social legislation that provided health, accident, disability and old-age pension insurance for workers. The system was funded through contributions made by the insured workers and their employers, and with government tax revenue. The system placed much emphasis on supporting workers in cases of accident or illness – until then, the costs of treatment by a physician or in hospital had been ruinously high for the working class.

Following the German example, trade unions and workers' movements in other European countries also succeeded in their struggle for the right to public social security in the late nineteenth and twentieth centuries.

After the Second World War, both private enterprises and the public sector had to be rebuilt. Governments played a central role in the recon-struction process, both in the communist countries of Eastern Europe and in Western Europe. In the post-war period, health systems across Europe experienced rapid growth and the numbers employed within the health sector outstripped population growth in most countries.

This situation began to change in the 1970s. Growth stagnated. The consensus about the contribution of the welfare state was jeopardised. There was a call for sharp reductions in public sector spending, particularly for labour-intensive services such as healthcare. In the 1990s most countries tried to 'reform' their health systems in order to reduce costs. Health service employees were confronted with continuous restructuring as a result of market-style reforms. They experienced work intensification, more precarious forms of employment status and job losses.

In 1948, the UK National Health Service (NHS) was established to provide to the entire population of the UK free healthcare at the point of delivery. Its aim was to treat all alike on the basis of need and not on the ability to pay. Charity and market-based provision had failed to deliver the universal healthcare that the nation required. In the 1930s only 43 per cent of the population were covered by the national insurance scheme. The NHS became a model for public services across much of the Western world. The architects of the NHS (for example, William Beveridge) recognised that equity in healthcare could only be achieved by sharing the risks and costs of care across the whole of society – from rich to poor and from healthy to sick. It is well-established that poverty and ill health are closely associated: the poor have higher rates of sickness and disease than the wealthy.

In the 1980s and 1990s, the Conservative government in the UK cut public expenditure and implemented a system of managed competition. The health services workforce declined by 55,000 between 1984 and 1994. Workloads increased and the number of hours of unrewarded overtime went up. Attempts to reduce the cost of cleaning services led to more cases of infections in hospitals. On the other hand, the number of general and senior managers in the privatised health sector grew rapidly (increasing from 4,600 to 22,900 between 1984 and 1994). Public spending on public services rebounded substantially after 1997 – by an average 6 per cent annually – under the Prime Minister, Tony Blair. Even so, health expenditure in the UK accounted for only 7.7 per cent of gross domestic product (GDP) in 2003, which is below the Organisation for Economic Cooperation and Development (OECD) average.

The countries of continental Europe also spend significant amounts on health, ranging from 7.7 per cent of GDP (Austria) to 11.2 per cent

(Switzerland) in 2002. The systems are typically funded, however, through employees' compulsory insurance contributions, with additional government support. In many cases, these insurance systems were established at a very early point (around 1900) in response to pressure from trade unions. Workers' dependants are also beneficiaries of the insurance system. Trade unions and employers' organisations continue to take an active part in shaping the insurance systems.

In Scandinavia, there is a long tradition of social security being regarded as a civil right. Every citizen is entitled to 'basic security benefits/services', with additional benefits for all those who are gainfully employed and thus integrated in the compulsory insurance system. Because tax money is the main source of funding for services and benefits, the level of taxation and government spending is comparatively high (approximately 50 per cent of GDP). The Scandinavian countries spend up to 10 per cent of GDP on health (Norway) and are among the states with the highest life expectancy figures worldwide.

One example is the tax-funded Swedish healthcare system. Services have been decentralised and provided by 26 local county councils. Each county council is responsible for the healthcare of its geographic area. Healthcare accounts for about 80 per cent of their total expenditure. Patients' fees are a minor component, about 2 per cent. And there is an annual maximum payment per patient of about US$250. Today, there are still only a handful of private hospitals concentrated in the main cities. And there is broad agreement on the necessity of a publicly organised and financed health system.

Financing of the health systems in Eastern Europe was initially modelled on the scheme introduced in the former Soviet Union in the 1920s, whereby health services were directly funded from the state budget. Planning and management were centralised. Healthcare professionals were paid by the state, generally at a rate below the average working wage. The Central and Eastern European (CEE) countries boast a number of establishments (hospitals, clinics and health centres) comparable to those in OECD countries. But medical and surgical equipment is on average more than 25 years old. A surplus of medical staff, combined with higher expenses for drugs, medical/surgical equipment and other supplies, will result in an enormous rise in costs. Health spending rates in the reform states of Central, Eastern and South-Eastern Europe (SEE) are the lowest in Europe today, with rates ranging from as little as 3.4 per cent of GDP in Albania to 8.3 per cent in Slovenia.

Most CEE and SEE countries have experienced a decline in their population's health status since the 1980s. Infant and maternal mortality are on the rise, along with deteriorating figures for male adults' life expectancy. The poor situation of physical and mental health is closely related to health-damaging environmental conditions, as well as income levels, the amount and quality of food available, the quality and availability of drinking water, heating and housing conditions. Russia, in particular, has seen a dramatic rise in the incidence of infectious diseases including syphilis, tuberculosis and AIDS; there is widespread malnutrition due to poverty and alcoholism. Life expectancy has dropped dramatically to 65 years.

Privatisation was tried out as an alternative, with the result that private spending on health has increased disproportionately, reaching 25 per cent or even more of total health spending in most CEE and SEE countries. The result is growing scepticism: in December 2004, 65 per cent of voters in Hungary rejected the privatisation of hospitals.


## North America

In the United States, hospitals are traditionally non-profit institutions, usually sponsored by a religious denomination. William Penn in Philadelphia started one of the earliest of these almshouses in 1713. These hospitals are tax-exempt as charities, but they do not provide the full range of medical care. They were supplemented by large public and private hospitals in major cities, as well as by research hospitals that are often affiliated with a medical school.

While the US health system is the most expensive worldwide, it is neither the best nor the most complete system. With an average US$5,000 per capita per year spent on health, the US health system eats up 14 per cent of GDP, which is more than in any other country. However, only 45 per cent of this is covered by public institutions; 30 per cent is covered by social insurance organisations, and some 25 per cent (an average per capita contribution of US$1,300 per year) is paid from the patients' pockets. For every visit to the doctor, 10–20 per cent of treatment costs are due, which is particularly hard on low-income families.

Much of the higher cost of the US system is a result of the much higher administrative burden resulting from the competing private agencies. Other factors include the high cost of medication and rapidly rising insurance premiums. Healthcare in the United States is a big business sector with a total volume of US$1,500 billion per year. Large companies like United Health select profitable treatments and patients by placing access restrictions on the services they offer. Wherever possible, those who are elderly, frail or at high risk of chronic illness are excluded from insurance or comprehensive health coverage. And United Health gains influence by spending millions of dollars every year on lobbying activities to ensure that the healthcare system remains a profitable and commercialised marketplace.

The US healthcare system is far from universal, with over 40 million people lacking insurance cover in 2001. The reason is that the US system is not based on compulsory public insurance. However, patients are entitled to medical care in the emergency rooms of hospitals. As many of these patients do not give their correct names, the federal, state and local governments have to pay enormous sums in support of the hospitals every year.

The US healthcare system is not the best worldwide: mortality rates are higher in the US than in most other OECD countries. The quality of health services has continued to decline and there has been an increase in infection rates and drug-resistant bacteria. This is partly due to a lack of health workers, especially nurses. There are also high levels of stress, safety risks and time pressure.

This contrasts with Canada, where there is still a national political consensus about healthcare as a public service. Canada spent 9.6 per cent of its GDP on healthcare in 2002. The Canadian public healthcare system was first introduced during the Great Depression of the 1930s. To provide affordable medical services to the impoverished sectors of the population, publicly financed medical examinations and health insurance were first introduced in the province of Saskatchewan. This was followed by the introduction of free healthcare for retirees in 1944 and of a public hospital system with very low fees in 1947. From 1964 on, this model was extended to cover all of Canada. In 1984, fees payable by patients were even legally banned.

## Latin America

For centuries, the countries of Latin America were colonies of European states that displayed little interest in social development. With the advent of independence and especially after the beginning of industrialisation in the nineteenth century, the most progressive Latin American states introduced public social services.

Economic and political crises during the past 30 years led to 'reforms' of the public sector. The overall aim of these reforms – executed under pressure from the World Bank and the International Monetary Fund – has been to increase the participation of the private healthcare sector and to reduce the public health sector. The trends were the destabilisation of the public health sector and the privatisation of the social security institutions and health services. Moreover, private health insurance expanded as national and international capital flowed in, and the role of the government shifted from healthcare provider to regulator. But such reforms often contributed to mounting crises.

Chile undertook the first privatisation of a public health system in 1981 under the military government which cut back drastically on the fiscal contribution to the public health system. As a result, the public system deteriorated sharply, health employment dropped and real wages in the sector declined. Workers were allowed to assign their mandatory payroll contributions for healthcare to private insurance plans. These plans are very profitable, primarily because they have successfully sought out the healthiest and higher-income segments of the population. The public service covers the less healthy, lower-income 75 per cent of the population. Since the restoration of democracy in Chile, the government has steadily increased the resources devoted to the public health system. But years of low investment have left deficits in infrastructure and human resources that have not yet been overcome.

A different health sector reform was launched in Colombia in the early 1990s. Prior to reform, health services were provided through a monopolistic social security system and private providers. According to estimates, less than 40 per cent of the population were covered by this scheme. The 1990s reform brought a communalisation of health services, a modernisation of health insurance and greater financial resources. Public health spending rose from 3.2 per cent of GDP in 1994 to 6.7 per cent in 2002. Public insurance coverage increased from 7.6 million people in 1994 to 21.7 million in 1997. Moreover, the reform generated about 18,000 new jobs. There were also positive effects on salary conditions. Today, life expectancy in Colombia is one of the highest in Latin America.

With an average 6.8 per cent of GDP, the Latin American and Caribbean region is spending more on health than most other continents. However, rates vary widely from state to state. Among the biggest problems of Latin America's healthcare systems today are the rising costs of AIDS and the resurgence of infectious diseases such as tuberculosis and malaria. International pharmaceutical companies find themselves under growing pressure from the region, especially from Brazil, to supply affordable drugs for these conditions.

Another major problem is the migration of healthcare professionals. Especially in the Caribbean countries, the loss of large numbers of nurses to OECD countries every year has created staffing problems for hospitals.

## Africa

The African countries too were colonies of European powers for centuries in which they were economically exploited, with hardly any effort being made toward the promotion of development. When the colonial era ended in the mid-twentieth century, the African countries won independence, and their governments took on a major role in building the new nations. The most marked advances in health and life expectancy were made in countries with a strong state component in social and health services. Contrary to much conventional wisdom, a country does not necessarily have to be rich to improve the quality of life for the majority of people through the provision of public services, especially healthcare and basic education. Botswana and Mauritius, for example, where above-average resources have been allocated to public services, enjoy greater life expectancy today than the populations of countries with greater wealth but lower health spending, such as Namibia and South Africa.

Since the 1960s, life expectancy in the developing world has risen from 40 to 63 years, and child mortality (the death rate of children below the age of five) has dropped to one third of the previous levels. Despite these advances, a great number of Africans are still victims of poverty and disease. Severe illness is more widespread in Africa than anywhere else in the world. Out of 40 million persons suffering from HIV infections worldwide, 30 million live in Africa.

More than half of all African countries still spend less than 5 per cent of GDP on health; that is, their health spending is lower than the World Health Organisation (WHO) recommendation. Some countries on the continent, however – including Gambia, Malawi, South Africa, Uganda and Zimbabwe – have raised their health budgets to between 7 per cent and 10 per cent of GDP.

While basic healthcare is usually available in cities, rural areas are often without any services at all. Efforts to provide at least rudimentary healthcare to rural populations are made by private organisations, development agencies, religious communities and communal initiatives.

A number of African countries have suffered the adverse effects of 'health reforms' undertaken at the behest of the IMF and the World Bank. In Guinea, the introduction of user fees led to a 30 per cent decline in outpatient visits. The introduction of fees for visits to Kenyan outpatient health centres led to a 52 per cent reduction in such visits. After fees were suspended, visits rose by 41 per cent. Zambia also abolished healthcare fees – one of the first positive results of debt relief for African countries in 2005. The fees had originally been introduced in the early 1990s under pressure from the IMF and the World Bank. Since then, many poor people died because they could not afford healthcare. In Malawi, one of the effects of the deficient health system was a rise in maternal mortality in the 1990s. Since 2001, expenditure on health increased significantly. In villages in Gambia where insecticide was provided free of charge, mosquito net impregnation for malaria prevention was five times higher than in villages where charges were introduced.

When the government, headed by President Museveni, came to power in Uganda in 1986, it found a civil service that was ineffective and demoralised and lacked accountability. Corruption and abuse of office were widespread. The mission of the health service reform was to develop a public service that delivers timely, high-quality and appropriate services at the lowest possible cost to the nation. Hospitals were made the responsibility of the local district councils, which also provide primary healthcare facilities. The councils employ the staff at these facilities. In 2002, Uganda spent 7.4 per cent of its GDP on health, much more than many other African countries.

## Asia

Asia has rich and long medical traditions, in some cases going back thousands of years. As well as India, Sri Lanka and China, the Arab countries can look back on a history of outstanding medical services and hospitals. However, these traditions have not been able to maintain their leading position to this day.

Depending on the individual countries' levels of development, health systems and health spending rates vary widely across the Asian continent today.

In China, the country with the largest population worldwide, the first network of social services for workers was built after the 1949 revolution. It covered illness and accidents and provided medical care for childbirth and maternity leave, disability and old-age pension benefits, as well as other social services. The provision of services was organised via the collectivised state enterprises. When the collectives were dismantled and the economic system reorganised along market economy lines from the early 1980s, healthcare became an expensive item for the majority of the Chinese. Currently, 80 per cent of the rural population are without insurance cover and have to pay their own way in case of illness. Less than 15 per cent of the workforce in China has medical insurance. About half of all Chinese do not go to the doctor when they are ill because they cannot afford to. Many hospitals have been privatised and are managed so as to generate profits.

Health sector deficiencies are also found in India. The world's second most populous nation has succeeded in raising life expectancy considerably over the last 25 years (from 50 to 61 years between 1970 and 1993) and has halved infant mortality rates. Nevertheless, life expectancy is still low in comparison to other nuclear powers. The Indian health system has a private sector with outpatient treatment and private clinics that provide nearly 80 per cent of all health services. Most doctors are concentrated in the private sector, and drugs are readily available as a rule. However, patients must pay for treatment immediately and in cash. The public sector provides basic healthcare in government clinics, family planning programmes and epidemics control. Healthcare is the responsibility of the individual states that receive additional funding from the federal government for specific programmes. An increasing problem is that India exports large numbers of doctors seeking better remuneration.

## Present Situation

Advances in health during the past few decades are impressive. The increase in life expectancy and the decrease in fertility throughout the world have been greater in the past 40 years than during the previous 4,000 years. Life expectancy is almost 25 years higher today than at similar income levels in 1900. Historical records show that the massive build-up of public healthcare systems with access for everyone has been the key to improving people's living conditions.

### High Public Health Spending Equals High Life Expectancy

Developed countries spend an average 7–10 per cent of GDP, or US$1,500 to US$2,000 per capita per year, on health systems. In 2002, the top spenders were the US (over US$5,000 per capita), followed by Switzerland

and Norway (over US$4,000). Countries in the developed world have two to four physicians and four to six hospital beds per 1,000 inhabitants. Most health spending in these countries comes from public institutions: public social insurance systems based on the principle of solidarity that cover illness, accident, the need for nursing care, and so on; government institutions; and local authorities. However, there is a discernible trend towards private health and accident insurance. In Europe, an average 66 per cent of health spending came from public sources in 2003; only 34 per cent was private spending. By contrast, patients/insured persons in the US and in Latin America on average have to pay more than 50 per cent of the health bill.

Life expectancy is highest in the OECD member states and in some countries in Central and South America, with an average lifespan of 75 years or more. Of the world's top 36 countries with respect to life expectancy, 19 are located in Europe and another five within the OECD. However, one factor that impacts negatively on life expectancy in the developed world is the rising trend towards obesity. There are already more overweight people worldwide than there are victims of malnutrition – a result of the unequal distribution of food.

Less developed countries spend an average 1–3 per cent of GDP on their healthcare systems, whereas the WHO recommends that developing countries spend a minimum of 5 per cent of GDP on health. In absolute figures, per capita health spending in less developed states amounts to US$10 or less annually. One case in point is Burundi, where recent figures put annual per capita health expenditure at no more than US$3 – a seemingly insuperable difference compared to developed countries. However, neighbouring Tanzania (US$13) and Uganda (US$18) have managed to invest substantially larger sums in public health. In developing countries, patients have to bear most of the financial burden of healthcare themselves. In sub-Saharan Africa, the privately paid share of the bill is typically 60 per cent or even higher.

Africa is the continent with the lowest average life expectancy; in most African countries, the average human lifespan is less than or just above 50 years. The main reason for this is high perinatal and infant mortality due to lack of medical services, combined with high levels of water-borne diseases. In countries with low life expectancy, one in four children dies before the age of five, while the corresponding figure for countries with higher life expectancy is one in 200. In less developed countries, 1–2 per cent of mothers die during or after childbirth, in developed countries the rate is only one in 20,000. Adequate medical services could save the lives of three out of four newborn babies and of innumerable women.

## More Public Services Equals Better Health

The incidence of diseases such as cholera and tuberculosis is directly related to the lack of public services, including investment in infrastructure to provide drinking water, sanitary wastewater disposal and basic healthcare. More than 2.6 billion people – over 40 per cent of the world's population – have no access to basic sanitary facilities, and more than 1 billion take their drinking water from contaminated sources. Over 50 per cent of Africans suffer from diseases that spread via contaminated water, such as cholera and infant diarrhoea. Health and education levels are closely linked: children's vaccination rates are more than 50 per cent higher if their mothers have received school education compared to those whose mothers have never attended school. AIDS spreads twice as quickly among girls without school education as among those who have received at least elementary schooling. Children have a 40 per cent higher chance of survival if their mothers have received five years of elementary schooling as compared with the children of mothers who have not gone to school.

More often than not, the problem is not so much finance as the setting of priorities. Developing and transitional countries ruled by authoritarian regimes spend much more on the military and police than on social and health services. David Hall from the Public Services International Research Unit (PSIRU) has demonstrated that the proportions are reversed in developed countries.[*]

---

[*] Wendy Caird, 'Where Will the Money Come From?', in *Focus on the Public Service*, 3/2005, Public Services International, p. 28.

## Privatisation: No Improvement in Health Services

The health sector has evolved into one of the biggest 'industries' worldwide. Global health spending has reached the level of US$3 trillion, about 8 per cent of global GDP. Since the 1980s and 1990s, the Reagan and Thatcher era, the world has witnessed a growing willingness to experiment with market approaches in the social sectors (health, education and social protection).

Hospitals have been sold into private ownership. Multinational healthcare management companies take over the running of public hospitals and run them as profit-makers rather than services. Cleaning, cooking, laundry and nursing services are handed over to private companies; private associations and societies have become active in the care of the elderly. But if complications arise, patients find themselves rapidly transferred to a public facility, because complications are inherently unprofitable.

The majority of these 'reforms' do not aim at improving services, but only at cutting costs. Employees and patients bear the brunt of these cost-cutting policies: the former may have to accept lower incomes, poor working conditions or outright redundancies; the latter are often discharged from hospital at the earliest possible point, to be taken care of by their families.

Private sector healthcare institutions are run in line with market criteria and are difficult to control by public supervisory agencies. They fail to cover regional supply gaps or specific needs. Expensive medical services remain within the public domain, while less cost-intensive, potentially profitable services are transferred to the private sector. Market-organised finance covers only that portion of the population able to pay premiums or direct user fees. Existing rules and standards for the protection of worker and patient health and safety are discarded to maximise profits.

## Liberalisation: Draining Health Professionals Away from Where They are Needed

The health sector is an important provider of jobs, employing as it does millions of people. Liberalisation and privatisation have resulted in a worldwide migration by healthcare service personnel such as doctors and nurses from developing and transitional countries to developed countries. The resulting decline in human resources in their countries of origin entails the danger of more overwork and higher ratios of patients to staff, while the increased labour supply in richer countries slows improvements in pay and working conditions there.

One example is sub-Saharan Africa, which now needs 620,000 more nurses to tackle the HIV/AIDS epidemic and meet basic UN development goals. The Philippines is the world's biggest exporter of such labour. It sends 14,000 nurses abroad each year – twice as many as it trains – but not to poor countries like those of sub-Saharan Africa. Britain recruits about 15,000 foreign nurses a year. Almost 25 per cent of physicians in Canada, Australia and the US are trained abroad.

## Health 'Reforms' have Failed

Globalisation has reduced the chances of less developed countries to build a functioning health system. Policies that attempt to solve governments' financial problems through budget cuts in health and social services and reduction of development aid funds create grave negative impacts. In particular, these cuts exacerbate existing imbalances in the distribution of wealth, both within societies and between world regions. Governments should ensure adequate funding of healthcare, based on the principle of solidarity, to prevent health services from becoming a privilege reserved for only a few. This means that all citizens should contribute to the funding of the social security system to the extent that they are able.

The ultimate test of the efficiency of health expenditure is the level of public health. If serious mistakes are made, the consequences can harm a society for decades, or even generations.

And after more than two decades of 'health reforms' the results are:

- a minimum of 1.3 billion people worldwide have no access to basic healthcare because there are not enough health professionals

- a shortfall of more than 4 million physicians, nurses, midwives, managers and other staff in the public health systems of the 57 poorest countries, 36 of which are in Africa
- 11 million children under the age of five die each year, most from easily preventable causes
- 18 of the poorest countries worldwide (with a total population of 460 million) are worse off today than they were 15 years ago. In all of them, incomes are declining, poverty is on the rise, and life expectancy figures are going down.

## International Organisations: Who Helps and Who Doesn't

With the adoption of the Millennium Declaration in September 2000, the members of the United Nations committed themselves to actively improving maternal health by 2015 and to combating HIV/AIDS, malaria and other transmissible diseases.

The WHO has made the same commitments. But in 1998, a WHO resolution for promoting public health over commercial interests was rejected as a result of industry lobbying. Large transnational corporations (TNCs) send more delegates to international WHO forums than most governments.

The interests of TNCs are supported primarily by the IMF, the World Bank and the World Trade Organisation (WTO). The World Bank urges governments to promote greater competition in the financing and delivery of health services. The whole purpose of the WTO's General Agreement on Trade in Services (GATS) is to promote international trade; it does not focus on other issues such as equity and fairness for consumers of health services, nor on labour considerations of those supplying the services.

## PSI and the Programme for Health and Social Services

PSI is most active on behalf of employees in the health sector. Working conditions in health services have deteriorated in a number of countries in the course of reform processes. Motivation and commitment erode quickly if staffing shortages push employees into constant overwork at poor pay. Healthcare workers are particularly exposed to stress and violence since they often deal with people in distress. Moreover, sexual harassment is a major problem for the large share of female health workers. At the same time, health sector employees are a vulnerable group because they rarely defend their interests through strikes that might endanger human lives.

In many countries, the health services are the largest single employer in the public sector. Thus, the largest single group of members within PSI are health workers – in recent years, 50 per cent of all new members have come from the health sector. There are now 230 affiliated unions representing health workers, with approximately 7 million members out of a total of 640 affiliates. For reasons that combine the members' interests and development principles, PSI defines health sector support as one of its core areas of activity.

In its global Programme for Health and Social Services (1993), PSI committed itself to supporting public health and working to avoid social hardship and marginalisation, stating that 'the health system structures must not be determined by the economic interests of private service providers'. The objective of the programme is to develop, expand and ensure comprehensive, free-of-charge public health service for everyone. A comprehensive public health system has to cover the need for outpatient and inpatient healthcare services, in particular in the following areas:

- combating infant mortality and improving maternal health
- AIDS education
- education for worker health and safety
- hospital and general care that meets the people's needs
- follow-up and outreach care programmes (rehabilitation, nursing care, integration of sick and disabled persons into society).

Social services have to include assistance to workers and their families, affording them protection against risks such as accident, disease and disability, and ensuring adequate care and income for these contingencies.

Occupational health and safety services have to reduce dangers to human health in the workplace.

Health sector employees have to be motivated in their work by participation in decision-making processes and their living and working conditions must be improved. PSI firmly opposes the health-threatening expansion of the workload that results from job sharing and personnel cuts. Humane working conditions and high-quality care for patients have to take priority over short-term rationalisation measures aimed exclusively at cost-cutting.

This PSI Programme was followed by a PSI Programme of Action for Health Services adopted by the 1997 PSI World Congress. PSI's health work is now conducted through the Health Services Task Force (HSTF) that is made up of health sector union representatives from all four regions. The HSTF advises the PSI Executive Board on all health-related matters and helps shape future policy developments in this area. In recent years, PSI has successfully conducted important campaigns against HIV/AIDS, for more nurses, for safety at work, for health sector reforms in consultation with workers and against the excessive migration of health workers and the protection of the rights of these workers.

# 8

# Social Services

## Historical Development

Security is one of the most basic human needs. Protecting oneself against life's misfortunes – accidents, illness, unemployment, old age – and their existentially threatening consequences has been and will continue to be a major concern for workers. For thousands of years, people have primarily looked to their families for help in such situations, as they still do in many regions of the world. In ancient Greece and Rome there were burial societies to which people contributed regularly to ensure that upon their death they would be buried with dignity. Some medieval guilds had programmes under which members contributed to funds that were drawn upon when members were no longer able to work, or died. As Christianity spread, Church institutions took up charitable works.

The concept of social security was born in France during the Age of Enlightenment. It figures in the Declaration of the Rights of Man and of the Citizen of 1789, whose Article 2 states: 'The aim of all political association is the preservation of the natural and imprescriptible [that is, inviolable] rights of man. These rights are liberty, property, security, and resistance to oppression'.

As industrialisation progressed in the early nineteenth century, mass poverty and miserable living conditions prevailed in the fast-growing cities, especially in Europe. Calls for social security systems marked the beginning of the workers' movement. The first social security systems were introduced to ameliorate the consequences of work-related accidents and income loss resulting from illness, disability or old age. Such systems were established in most of today's developed countries of Western and Northern Europe, in North America, Australia and New Zealand in the period before the

First World War, in most cases in response to pressure from the workers' movement and the trade unions.

Social protection laws were first introduced by a number of authoritarian regimes to curb unrest among revolutionary workers and undercut the socialist movement. In the interwar period (1919–39), democratic governments were particularly active in the further development of social policy. Beginning in the 1930s and 1940s, the Scandinavian countries and Britain in particular established broad social service systems that also offered assistance in such fields as childcare and housing.

The first social programmes did not cover the entire population but only wage earners. In particular, industry workers were the first group to be included in government-sponsored social insurance schemes. Over the course of the twentieth century, coverage was gradually extended to workers in small- and medium-sized trade and commerce sectors and in agriculture, and to self-employed persons and women.

## What are Social Services?

The broad view of health and social services is important as it underlines their true role of providing security. They are the means through which many social objectives can be realised: equality of opportunity, the provision of financial security for periods of sickness, unemployment, old age and child-rearing, housing, and employment services. So social services are mostly defined to include social work services, accommodation/housing services, labour market and employment/unemployment services, retirement schemes, income maintenance schemes, social security, social insurance and community services.

Social services can mean very different things. In Britain, for example, the 'personal social services' are particularly associated with social work ('case work'). In some countries social workers have powers over housing and social security provision; in other countries they do not. In some countries, social workers are employed by the state; in others, like the Netherlands, they are primarily employed by non-state private welfare agencies.

In many countries, volunteers and voluntary organisations play an important role in helping particular groups. Some organisations may even receive public funding to carry out some of their activities and enjoy special fiscal status. But their continuity is not secure and their public accountability is doubtful. They are selective in the groups that they assist. There are many unpaid caregivers: for example, in many societies women spend much of their life caring for parents or other dependants in addition to caring for their children.

The last few decades have seen the emergence of for-profit organisations in the field. Many of them are able to compete only because they pay low wages, offer little job security and frequently use part-time, temporary or casual staff without proper training or experience.

## Why They Became Public Services

How social services are structured differs from place to place, particularly according to local, regional and national government structures. Strategic aspects of economic, social and political activity have often been taken under the wing of the public authorities. These activities were either neglected (because they were financially unattractive) or were too attractive (and lucrative) to be left in private hands and thus rendered vulnerable to speculation. Over the centuries, the state sector has tended to grow, because economic and social life has become more complex and because democracy, as an ideal and a process, has been widely seen as the right path to take. Collective decision-making, collective accountability and collective responsibility are an integral part of democracy. And this collective activity is most equitably carried out by properly accountable public bodies.

## Europe

European countries have developed the highest levels of social services in the world. Social services in most countries of the European Union (EU) are currently provided by the public sector, in some by non-profit and commercial organisations. The EU countries usually spend 20–30 per cent of GDP on social services and social security.

The Nordic welfare model is unique in many respects. In Scandinavia, social security has traditionally been regarded as a civil right. Everyone is entitled to the same basic level of security, and those in employment receive additional benefits under compulsory insurance schemes. In addition to generous social benefits aimed at income maintenance, the Nordic systems offer a broad range of public social services. Tax revenues are an important component in financing the welfare state, with comparatively high levels of taxation and state expenditure. The only area outside the public sphere is unemployment insurance, which is managed by the trade unions.

Critics of the welfare state in Scandinavia have argued for decades that the growth of the public sector has caused stagnation in the growth of the overall economy because increasing taxation crowds out private investments and private entrepreneurship. But even during the 1990s crises, labour productivity was higher in the Scandinavian countries than the EU and US average. This makes it clear that social security and business are not incompatible phenomena like fire and water. Thus, attitudes among the great majority of the Scandinavians have remained solidly in support of most social programmes.

The outstanding characteristics of the Scandinavian type of welfare state are its work-, women- and family-friendliness – essential preconditions for women's integration in the labour force. Even though more women have paid jobs in Sweden than elsewhere, they have more children than women in most other European countries. Many ingredients of Sweden's family policy are totally lacking in most other countries; for example, advances on unpaid child maintenance, paternity leave and contact days.

Most countries in Europe offer some form of economic assistance to families with children. The two main channels are cash handouts and tax relief. Cash payments vary greatly from country to country. They may be payable to all or only to members of the workforce or to those belonging to a given trade union. The same amount may be payable to all or it may vary in proportion to income or be means-tested. The trend in a number of countries is towards reducing general allowances for families with children and instead focusing on those who are worst off. A number of countries offer different forms of tax relief, but there is now a tendency for the scope of this form of assistance to be reduced.

The fact that there is a growing need for care for the elderly is a relatively new discovery even in Europe, and many countries still do not acknowledge that this is a public matter. But a growing number of working people do not have enough time to care for their parents. The ways in which care for old people is organised and financed vary widely, making it difficult to draw an accurate picture of services for older people in Europe. As a back-up to the help provided by the family, various forms of day centres and organised home help for older and disabled people have evolved in most countries of Western Europe. Local governments, church groups, voluntary organisations or private service providers may provide these services. Even the forms of financing vary, ranging from funding via taxation pure and simple, to gifts/charity, to user charges in various hybrid forms. Most countries have organised home nursing for the elderly provided in their own homes. In this instance, too, there are different ways in which the services are organised. All countries have special forms of institutional accommodation with integrated care and nursing facilities for older people needing a lot of care. The responsible authorities and modes of financing vary from country to country and also within countries.

Social security networks are least developed in the countries of Southern and Eastern Europe. In Southern Europe, the family still plays an important social role in providing security for its members. Nor is the state the main source of income maintenance in Southern Europe; corporate funds, the church and the social partners fulfil this function. In the former Soviet Union and in communist Eastern Europe, most social benefits and services were provided via the state-owned enterprises. This system collapsed almost completely as a result of privatisation and the economic crises of the early 1990s, and governments were in many cases unable to establish functioning substitutes. The initial optimism over the end of communism quickly turned to disillusionment for many.

The past 30 years have seen major changes in the way both healthcare and social services are provided in Europe. In some countries we have seen a move away from the state as service provider to third-sector organisations or private businesses – as was the case in the UK and in the countries of

Eastern Europe. There has been a move out of large institutions and into services delivered in primary and community settings.

Today, there are wide differences between European countries in levels of inequality and relative poverty. An estimated 50 million people even in Europe are still or again experiencing social exclusion: this means lack of education, deteriorating health conditions, homelessness, loss of family support, non-participation in the regular life of society, and lack of job opportunities.

## The Americas

'All that harms labour is treason to America,' said US President Abraham Lincoln.[*] Since the time of the nineteenth-century Settlement House Movement, workers have argued for a focus on the systemic causes of poverty and social reform.

In the United States, public social security systems were first developed in the Great Depression era of the 1920s and 1930s, when hundreds of thousands of First World War veterans and millions of unemployed lived in abject poverty. To cover the most basic needs, public health and pension systems were introduced, as well as unemployment insurance. President Franklin Delano Roosevelt's New Deal, launched in 1933, was an economic and social reform package that included heavy government investment, a massive reduction of working hours (to 30 hours), progressive taxation (that is, low taxes for the poor, high taxes for the rich) and a social insurance system. Since the time of the New Deal, political debate in the US has always revolved around the opposing positions of regulation and deregulation of the economy, with a trend towards deregulation in the 1980s. Today, the US spends 15 per cent of its GDP on social security.

In Latin America, high-quality social security systems already existed early in the twentieth century in several highly developed countries, such as Argentina, Chile and Brazil. Over the last decades, however, developments were reversed as a result of profound political and economic crises, in many

---

[*]  As quoted in 'Union Goes on Legal Offensive', *Focus on Public Services*, 2/2006, Public Services International, p. 20.

cases exacerbated by social policy cutbacks mandated by the IMF and the World Bank. Today, Latin America is the region with the greatest income disparities worldwide. Social systems are insufficient in terms of coverage, do not address poverty effectively and are chronically underfunded. Black and indigenous people have only restricted access to social services.

## Asia and the Pacific

In Asia, the family is generally still responsible for ensuring the well-being of all its members. Social spending has reached significant levels only in the highly developed countries of the region (17 per cent of GDP in Japan, around 18 per cent of GDP in Australia and New Zealand).

## Social Services Today

Social protection coverage today is most extensive in developed regions such as Europe, while developing countries and regions such as Africa, parts of Asia and Latin America have the least coverage.

Neoliberalism has caused immense harm to social services in the last few decades and continues to do so. Neoliberals set out to devalue the state and the agencies that work on its behalf, especially social services. Social services have been widely portrayed as creating and perpetuating social problems rather than solving them. They would not empower, but stifle, personal freedom and restrict economic growth. 'Get big government off my back' and the 'nanny state' were slogans to get across the idea that public services encourage dependence, even idleness. And those who receive state help are demonised as being basically parasitic. One of neoliberalism's chief spokespersons and executors, Margaret Thatcher, even claimed that 'there is no such thing as society, there are just individuals'. In focusing on individual achievement, the implication was clearly made that unemployment is the fault of the unemployed. Unemployment would be caused by workers 'pricing themselves out of the market', because social services are too expensive.

Right-wing politicians have set about restructuring and demolishing social services and cutting back the resources. But at the same time that resources were going down, the demands on social services have gone up. The number of clients of social services has increased dramatically in many countries since the onset of economic recession. About 30 per cent of the world's workers cannot find productive employment; 195 million have no work at all. They and their families make up the vast bulk of the 1.1 billion poor who have to try and survive on less than US$1 per day. The 'temporary slowdown' of social services very easily becomes a permanent decline. Once started, it is virtually impossible to reverse, as the gap between what is and what should be becomes ever greater.

On a global scale, poverty rates (people living on less than US$1 per day) decreased from 40 per cent in 1981 to 21 per cent in 2001. But in Latin America they did not come down, and in sub-Saharan Africa they even increased from 42 per cent to 47 per cent. Even Europe and Central Asia saw rises from 1 per cent to 4 per cent.

Resourcing social services has to be seen not as a short-term cost, but as a long-term investment – an investment to prevent the adverse economic, political and social consequences that inevitably erupt in an uncaring and brutalising society. The problem is not a lack of resources – they are abundantly available – but the setting of priorities. There is a clear negative correlation between public police and private security expenditures and expenditures for social services.

With services stretched beyond their limits, it is imperative that a concerted international offensive be mounted to promote and restore the fundamental ideals of collective social action.

The state's role of being the final 'safety-net' is certain. At some point in their lives, everyone will have need of social services. But it is wholly unrealistic to promote the idea that the individuals should be responsible for making their own personal provisions. Many people do not – 40 million US citizens without health insurance prove it.

Therefore, the state should be fully responsible for the planning, commissioning and regulating of social services, whether or not services are provided directly by the public sector. Private social services cannot guarantee that people will actually have access to desired or necessary services at an affordable cost when they need them. This requires very robust systems with clear service standards, systems of monitoring and transparent lines of accountability.

Social services work best when their system of financing is compulsory. Compulsory, that is, when people are in employment rather than in retirement, unemployed, disabled, homeless or destitute. The level of contributions has to take into account the wealth and income of individuals and commercial undertakings.

The main asset of social services is the people who work in them. Improving the quality of social services depends to a large extent on investing in human resources. These investments have to be made in terms of pay, conditions of work and employment, training and qualifications and the promotion of equal opportunities. No organisation is better placed to care for this than PSI. PSI's principles regarding public service have remained consistent over time, although at every congress they have been refined to keep pace with events. In 1972, PSI set up a Health and Social Services section that has met regularly since, although in a much-altered form. As a result of these meetings, the World Congress adopted a World Policy Programme for the Health Service in 1985. In 1991, the Health and Social Services Committee decided to integrate social services into the Policy Programme. PSI is fighting for social services that:

- prevent poverty rather than only relieving poverty once it has arisen
- provide genuine security against contingencies such as unemployment, sickness, old age, disability and homelessness
- meet the needs of everyone, on the basis of adequate benefits paid as a right
- act as one of a number of means of sharing out resources more fairly by distributing income both between social groups and over the lifecycle of individuals
- are part of an overall social provision, combined with policies to tackle unemployment, low pay, healthcare, education and housing
- treat people as individuals, recognising and respecting their particular needs

- recognise society's collective responsibility for children and others in need of care
- allow equal access and provide equal treatment to everyone regardless of race, marital status or sexual orientation
- are administered efficiently and courteously
- provide benefits which are easy to understand and to administer
- are accountable to users and to those who work in them
- act as model employers, treating their own staff fairly on the basis of the above principles where relevant.

# 9

# Pensions

Not having to work in old age, but not having to go begging either – this was and still is what many people dream of. In many countries of the world, the family has for thousands of years taken care of old members no longer able to work. But as younger people began to move to the cities in increasing numbers, this form of care for the elderly gradually ceased to function. As a result, other provisions have had to be made to prevent poverty. Today, more than half of all people worldwide live in cities, but their hopes for jobs and sufficient incomes often remain unfulfilled. Providing financial support and care for the elderly has increasingly turned into a service of public interest.

## Historical Development

Pensions were originally paid by rulers to followers who did not have sufficient independent incomes from property or other sources. Armies were among the first organisations to pay pensions – in this case as a reward to veterans (for example, the Royal Navy in 1693).

As industrialisation progressed in the nineteenth century, survival in old age became an ever more urgent problem for workers. Three basic approaches were developed to solve the problem: compulsory insurance based on the insured person's contributions, fully government-funded systems, and government-subsidised systems. Broadly speaking, most countries of the world follow one of these three approaches today.

## The Anglo-American approach to pensions

Countries following the Anglo–American approach tend to have a minimal, usually flat-rate, basic pension run by the state and financed out of its current revenue. State expenditure on pensions in these countries tends to be low. In Australia, state-financed basic pensions were introduced in 1908. The UK introduced this pension scheme in 1911; its total expenditure – 5 per cent of GDP – is among the lowest in the EU and the OECD. The US introduced it in 1935 and spends 4 per cent of GDP on it.

To supplement the basic pension, and in some cases to minimise or even replace it, countries tend to encourage significant supplementary schemes. They are run by private sector financial institutions (banks, insurance companies, pension funds and other fund managers). They usually invest individuals' and employers' contributions in the stock markets, hoping that the investment returns will be sufficient to pay out pensions. Such a funded system may be organised on an occupational (company), industry-wide, national or individual basis, and may be compulsory or voluntary. This model is promoted most avidly by the US and the UK, most of the Eastern European countries (where public pensions are very low), Australia, Chile, South Africa, Canada and Japan. Two thirds of the world's largest pension funds have their headquarters in the US.

## The European Form of Solidarity

Public pay-as-you-go pension systems have been an important social policy building block in Europe for about the last 100 years. The first scheme along these lines was introduced in Germany in 1889. The underlying consensus that old age should not imply the threat of poverty is one of the underlying tenets of the European welfare state. Practically every old person receives a pension that provides a more or less sufficient income. In most European countries, pension systems are the social protection programme that receives the widest attention. On average, 12 per cent of GDP – more than in any other part of the world – is spent on old-age pension benefits. Many European countries have a large basic pension, frequently with an earnings-related component, run by the state. Pensions are paid out of current social insurance, taxation, and public expenditure – a public pay-as-you-go system. This continental European model is in place in most countries of the EU.

Corporate pension schemes have become the most important supplementary form of private pension investment in most EU countries – 100 of the world's 300 biggest pension funds are managed by and for employees of major European enterprises. In a number of countries, companies are directly or indirectly mandated to establish retirement schemes; in others, they can freely decide whether or not to run pension plans. In countries where trade unions have been influential in designing corporate pension systems, the systems contain elements of solidarity. Moreover, most EU countries offer fiscal incentives for corporate and individual pension investments. There is, however, little public and no corporate co-funding for individual private pension investments. Because private pension funds have spread from the US and the UK to Central and Eastern Europe in recent years, the European model of solidarity is increasingly on the defensive.

## Latin America

In Latin America, public pension systems were also set up at an early point when traditional family care for the elderly began to disappear as a result of industrialisation. As early as 1888, Brazil adopted a pension scheme for the workers of the national railways. In Argentina, pensions for public servants were introduced in 1904. Most other countries in the region followed suit in the 1920s and 1930s, and many leading political figures owed their popularity to these social reforms. As a consequence of the economic downturn and soaring inflation rates of the 1970s, most pension systems were hit by financial difficulties. Additional pressure came from the World Bank which made financial assistance dependent on governments' willingness to cut down public expenditure. In effect, it dictated the transition to capital-funded schemes.

In Chile, the dictator Augusto Pinochet destroyed one of the region's oldest and best-working systems in 1981. The system, which had previously covered the majority of workers, was replaced by more or less private pension funds to which only workers had to contribute – neither employers nor the government made contributions. Likewise, a partial transition to a funded system was made in Argentina in 1994. The resulting situation, in which benefit accruals have to be settled by the government – that is, paid from public monies – while contributions flow into private pension funds, has created public deficits which were a contributing factor to the financial collapse of 2002.

The Latin American countries spend only 2 per cent of GDP on average on old-age pensions, the second-lowest figure among all continents. Survival has become more difficult for elderly people over the last few decades, as they receive no or only very small pensions. Over 50 per cent of women in most countries will not receive pensions because they have spent their lives as homemakers without paid employment. Women subsidise a system that excludes them. Any reforms promoting the private pensions sector will only exacerbate the gender and poverty gap in old age.

## The Asia-Pacific Model

The Asian-Pacific model is dominated by state-run and state-funded pension schemes, usually referred to as national or central provident funds. They tend to provide extensive or universal coverage for a country's workforce and invest heavily in government securities. The Asian model combines elements of both Anglo-American and European approaches. Like the Anglo-American model, it is dominated by funded investment schemes. But these schemes are run publicly, rather than privately. The model uses stock markets but does not depend on them.

The number of old-age pension beneficiaries as a percentage of the population varies as widely across countries as the levels of development and economic performance. Public spending on pensions is very low, amounting to 3 per cent of GDP. In past or present communist countries, spending rates are at the level of the Asian average. Pension expenditure is highest in the most developed countries of the region, such as Japan.

Traditionally, most elderly people in Asia have had to rely on the solidarity of their families. But as in other regions, migration to the cities, emigration to other countries and rising unemployment rates have eroded the traditional family support network.

Since the establishment of the People's Republic of China in 1949, industrial enterprises and agricultural collectives have paid pensions there. Over time, the growing number of pensioners created an economic burden, in particular on older enterprises. The problem became especially acute in the 1980s when large numbers of older workers were sent into retirement. Reform plans for a more balanced pension system foresee payroll-linked contributions by enterprises to an insurance that will pay out benefits. Chinese living in rural areas are even worse off, as the occupational pension system was completely abolished when agricultural enterprises were de-collectivised. So far, only about one third of China's regions have developed alternative systems. Pension benefits are quite small, barely covering the basic necessities of life, so that many elderly people become impoverished. This is one of the reasons why the family is still widely regarded as an important social support network. However, China's strict birth control policy (the one-child family) puts severe constraints on this function.

In India, support programmes for the elderly have been set up in a substantial number of states, especially those with strong workers' movements. Uttar Pradesh developed a general old-age pension system in 1957, and pension schemes for widows and for agricultural workers were introduced in Kerala in 1961. Tamil Nadu and Maharashtra followed suit. Current plans foresee a new funded system, with the gradual extension of coverage from public servants to the sub-continent's 300 million job-holders.

The most economically successful country in Asia, Japan is a latecomer in the social policy field. For many years, there was general consensus that economic development would have to come first, while social services would have to wait. As a result of fundamental reforms undertaken in 1986, all Japanese citizens aged 65 and above are entitled to a fixed public pension, regardless of prior employment. For self-employed persons and housewives, this grant is the only legal pension. Additional legal pension insurance for job-holders is managed via the employing companies, with contributions and benefits set in accordance with employees' income levels. Large corporations offer additional pension plans, in which the level of benefits depends on the number of years an employee has worked for the corporation. When an employee leaves the corporation, accruals are paid out either as severance pay or as a monthly supplementary pension.

## Africa

Africa is the region with the lowest levels of pension expenditure, ranging from as little as 0.1 per cent of GDP (for example, in Chad) to less than 1 per cent in most of the sub-Saharan states, to 2–3 per cent of GDP in the countries of northern and southern Africa. Persons over 60 and pension beneficiaries still make up a significantly smaller percentage of the population than in other regions of the world. Where old-age pension systems are in place, they usually cover only employees in public adminis-trations, the police or the military. In these cases, average pension benefits tend to be higher than the respective countries' average income levels. Those who are entitled to pension benefits often find it difficult to get their claims honoured.

It appears that in many African countries, providing for people's old age is still a largely neglected social policy area. But the number of potential beneficiaries is bound to increase sharply over the next decades. According to UN estimates, the number of people over 60 in Africa will increase five-fold, from 40 to 205 million, over the next 50 years. Public or semi-public old-age support systems will have to be introduced.

A positive example of reform efforts is found in Ghana: supported by economic development, a number of important innovations in the areas of health, old-age support and basic education have been introduced. Gabon has created a special social support scheme for elderly people who are not covered by pension systems. In Nigeria, the state-run pension funds were replaced by a pay-as-you-go system in response to notorious misuse of the funds' collected assets. Moreover, trade unions can directly or indirectly influence investment decisions and thus promote political freedom. New pay-as-you-go systems were also introduced in Angola, Mozambique and Zimbabwe.

## Privatisation of Old-Age Pension Systems

Social security systems have become major elements of social development in the twentieth century, with particularly important effects on the well-being of the older groups of society.

The situation changed in the early 1970s. The US abandoned controls on capital movements so that money could be moved into any investment promising higher returns. Since then, the World Bank and the IMF have pushed many countries into transforming their pension systems, adding supplementary corporate and individual capital market-based systems to public systems based on solidarity. The arguments were always the same: the ratio of paid workers to pensioners is declining. The public sector does not have enough money to pay out the pensions of increasing numbers of old people. States are already spending too much on pensions. If the state provides a reasonable public pension, people will not save and invest on their own. The private sector liberates people from dependence on the state. Future benefits would depend on the individual contribution to pension funds and not on political distribution considerations and measures.

Thus, 'pensions dollars' have fuelled the expansion of the world's financial markets. Global financial markets today rely substantially on private pension funds. Worldwide pension assets were estimated to be over US$12 trillion at the end of the 1990s. This was more than 40 per cent of world GDP. The need for cash to buy privatised firms has been a major argument for pension reform in Central and Eastern Europe. Private pension funds are the largest institutional holders of company shares.

But none of the arguments of the World Bank and the IMF hold up. Experience with private pension systems shows that the privatisation of pensions has led neither to higher pensions for more people, nor to greater economic growth. Former UN economist Larry Willmore said that 'social security reform in itself is not likely to generate increased savings or growth;

it is essentially a zero sum game in which some participants gain at the expense of others'.[*]

One need only look at Britain, once held up as a model by pension reformers, to see how the lofty ideals behind privatisation can easily go awry. The privatisation policies adopted during the era of Margaret Thatcher in the 1980s and 1990s have resulted in a drastic reduction of pension benefits and a significant increase in poverty. The incomes of approximately half of all pension beneficiaries have fallen below the poverty line. Between 85,000 and 125,000 people in the UK have already lost some or all of their private pensions because of corporate bankruptcies. After two decades of pension privatisation, it is private pensions rather than public ones that are showing signs of creaking. Under Tony Blair, the government responded by introducing tax credits for pensioners. The resulting income improvement helped boost consumption, stimulate growth and bring down unemployment rates.

## Secure Private Pensions? Not at All!

States are paying premiums for private pension schemes to provide a feeling of security. But at the turn of the millennium it became clear that private occupational pension schemes in the UK and the US were grossly underfunded. Worldwide, pension funds are today estimated to be 20 per cent underfunded, representing US$1.5–2 trillion. Some companies have holes in their pension plans larger than the value of the company itself. A November 2005 survey showed that more than one third of the UK's top 350 companies believed their businesses could be at financial risk because of company pension scheme deficits. Nevertheless, in 2004, the 100 biggest UK companies paid out four times as much in dividends to shareholders than in repairing holes in their pension schemes.

If stock market returns have nothing to do with real economic growth, then security in retirement becomes an illusion. What are their savings going to be worth if they have expanded without any equivalent expansion in the

---

[*]  L. Willmore, 'Social Security and the Provision of Retirement Income', mimeograph, United Nations, New York, 1998.

real economy, nationally or internationally? The *Financial Times* wrote (1 July 2005) that private pension schemes are 'a shameful confidence trick'.

## Little Benefit for Local Economies

Being 'successful' in stock market terms means being able to achieve dividends or capital gains. Many pension funds are doing nothing for local investment or for local demand for labour, goods and services. Overseas equities now account for about 45 per cent of the stocks and shares held by UK pension funds and insurance companies. And pension fund sales of UK equities have helped drive down UK share prices further, making UK companies more attractive to overseas investors. By 2005, overseas investors held over 32 per cent of the UK stock market. Thus, future pensioners may have a good rate of return in gross financial terms, but the production of local goods and services could well have declined; they may also have to pay more tax and support their unemployed children, their streets may be unsafe, and many local facilities may have closed.

## High Costs for the State

In the UK, the present system of private pensions is estimated to cost the state £21 billion a year in lost revenue. The reason is that contributions to private pensions have been largely tax exempt. In the US, the system has been estimated to cost the state US$ 50 billion a year.

The US government set up the Pension Benefit Guaranty Corporation (PBGC) in 1974 as an insurance scheme for company occupational pension schemes. In 2003, the Corporation was itself put on the list of institutions that might need a taxpayer bailout.

In the UK, the government's Pension Protection Fund (PPF) is modelled on the US PBGC. It was introduced in 2005 as a result of protest by contributors to pension funds that have been wound up, paying out little or no benefits, after the sponsoring companies went bankrupt.

The Confederation of British Industry is already calling for taxpayers to contribute to this pensions lifeboat.

## High Costs for Contributors

A significant proportion of the contributions to private pension funds are used to cover administrative costs. In 1990, the operating costs of the Chilean private pension funds accounted for 15 per cent of annual contributions. By 2000, half the contributions by Chilean workers who retired in 2000 went on management fees. In Argentina, administrative expenses eat up a staggering 36 per cent of contributions to private pension funds. In the UK, various fees and costs, explicit or implicit, have consumed an estimated 40–45 per cent of the value of individual private pensions. In Singapore, which has a public monopoly on pension provision, the operating costs are only 0.53 per cent of annual contributions and 0.1 per cent of total assets.

Switching from a pay-as-you-go public pension system to a funded one itself costs money. The generation making the switch has to pay twice. It has to pay the pensions of its parents' generation while at the same time setting aside savings to fund its own retirement.

## De-solidarisation of Workers

A private pension arrangement sensitises workers to financial issues and enterprise performance, reducing the dichotomy between capital and labour – but without advantages for the workers. The driving forces behind private pension schemes aim at the de-solidarisation of workers. They want to shift power from the public sector to private big business where there is little chance for democratic participation in decision-making processes.

## Too Many Old People? No, but Too Many Poor People!

Once upon a time our biggest fear was of dying too young. Now it is of living too long. Life expectancy in many countries has been rising for the past 200 years. But in Russia it has dropped significantly since 1985, especially for men. In sub-Saharan Africa, life expectancy has dropped precipitously by 10–20 years in the past two decades. The World Health Organisation predicts a surge in deaths around the world from diabetes, heart disease and cancer. And life expectancy is distributed unevenly across social groups: the average unskilled manual worker in the UK is likely, at the age of 65, to live to 78, whereas the average professional can expect to live another five years, to 83. In the US, white people live on average about five years longer than African-Americans.

Raising the retirement age at which people can begin to draw a pension assumes that there are jobs and training available. Today about 30 per cent of the world's workers cannot find productive employment; 195 million have no work at all. If there is a crisis of too many old people, it is one of too many people in poverty in their old age, both now and in the future. Problems of pension financing derive less from demographic changes than from unemployment, low wages, and a shift in income distribution away from wages towards corporate profits.

## Perspectives

Secure pensions are possible – if those in power want them. This is one of the goals of PSI. Of the 300 biggest pension funds worldwide – with total assets of about US$4 trillion – two thirds are for public sector workers. Private pension funds often pursue aggressive investment strategies that are a threat to jobs. Counter-strategies are needed to ensure respect for workers' rights. 'Through their unions, workers must exert greater control over these pension funds', PSI states in its 'Pensions Action Recommendations' that were adopted in The Hague in 2001. 'These companies do need a civilising influence from people who don't only focus on maximum profits … I don't want to get rich on the back of child labourers, or by polluting the environment, by supporting dictators or by denying workers their basic rights', said PSI General Secretary Hans Engelberts. An exchange of information about the investment behaviour of funds and, above all, negotiations with the funds are needed to ensure that workers' and human rights are respected when investment decisions are made, that investments are made in public infrastructure, and that women's concerns are taken into account.

America's biggest pension fund, CalPERS (California Public Employees Retirement System) constitutes a successful example of good practice. CalPERS covers 1.2 million government employees and manages assets of about US$150 billion. With the active support of PSI, the fund developed a new investment strategy that it began to implement in 2002. This strategy does not focus exclusively on economic factors, but also considers whether workers' and human rights, democracy and freedom of the press are ensured when making investment decisions. As a result, CalPERS does not invest in the Philippines, China, Pakistan, India, Indonesia, Egypt or Russia, among others.

# 10

# Water and Sewage

Water is not a commodity like any other. Lost woodland may be regained through reforestation, crude oil may be replaceable by solar energy, but there is no substitute for water, a resource that constitutes one of the basic elements of life. It is needed in all spheres of human life and is critical for the continued existence of the biosphere. Ensuring water supply is one of the fundamental tasks of any society.

At the same time, clean, drinkable water is a scarce commodity. While the world's population has doubled over the last 70 years, global water consumption has increased six-fold. Currently, about 54 per cent of renewable freshwater resources are used. Uneven distribution of resources and consumption is at the heart of the water issue. For example, China has 21 per cent of the world's population, but only 7 per cent of global freshwater resources. Households account for only 10 per cent of global water consumption, industry and commerce for another 20 per cent (some 400,000 litres of water are needed in the production of just one car), and the lion's share of 70 per cent is consumed in agriculture.

The minimum amount of water which one human being needs for drinking, washing, cooking, cleaning and sanitary purposes is about 50 litres per day. Clean water is the most important factor in the prevention of diseases such as typhoid, cholera, dysentery and diarrhoea. Currently, about one quarter of the world's population do not have sufficient access to clean water.

## Historical Development

The provision of clean water was seen as an important public task as long ago as in the developed civilisations of antiquity. Ramses the Great, Semiramis and King Solomon are credited with the construction of the oldest known aqueducts. In China, irrigation ditches were built to transport water to rice paddies. Greece was the first country in which water was brought into the cities from distant sources through subterranean transport lines. The aqueducts of ancient Rome are among the most important structures built at that time. In Latin America, the Inca Empire also developed a public water supply system.

Drainage ditches were built as early as 3000 BC in the cities of the Euphrates valley to remove rainwater and prevent flooding. Open sewers of this type were also in use in Roman times. The understanding of the important sanitary function of communal sewer systems was lost in the early Middle Ages, however, which led to devastating cholera and plague epidemics that kept recurring for centuries.

The rapid growth of cities in the modern era necessitated the introduction of organised water and wastewater management systems. Vienna was the first European city with a complete sewer system in 1739. In London, private water supply was replaced by a public system of water pipelines early in the nineteenth century, after three catastrophic cholera epidemics had claimed 30,000 lives. Up until that period, the River Thames had been used as an open sewer, but from 1842 on, a system of sewers was built which drained wastewater to collecting basins outside the city. By the twentieth century, public water supply and wastewater management systems were recognised as hallmarks of a progressive society.

With the ascendancy of neoliberalism, public water supply systems came under attack. In the UK, the deregulation and privatisation wave of the Thatcher era hit the water supply systems in the 1980s, and the British example found many imitators worldwide. The concepts of business admin-istration – 'increasing efficiency', 'necessary concentration processes', 'more competition', 'economies of scale', and others – were introduced in the debate and presented as though there were no alternatives.

The world's liberalised and privatised water markets, however, are dominated by only three big players: the French Suez and Veolia groups (the former has 120 million customers worldwide, the latter about 100 million) and Thames Water (about 70 million customers). The big three have been involved in most privatisations around the world in recent years and have managed to reverse the earlier domination of US corporations, pushing the latter back to their home markets. Real competition between these large industrial groups happens at best during tender processes. Once a sales deal is agreed or a licence granted, they no longer have to fear any competition. They have frequently tried to alter the terms of a deal after conclusion of the agreement, and in many cases Veolia and Suez even share water supply licences or cooperate in specific areas.

When the wave of privatisations and private licensing reached its crest in the 1990s, many corporations focused on the developing world and Eastern Europe. In the countries of the South, the big players usually supply water only in big cities where maximum profits can be earned at minimum cost. As a result, rural areas have been largely neglected. Providing water and wastewater disposal to the poor is not an attractive business for private-sector companies. And everywhere, privatisation has resulted in often substantial water price increases. This has triggered popular protests, eventually leading to the re-communalisation of water supply systems in a significant number of cases.

After the failure of many privatisations, even a 2005 World Bank study stated that there is 'no statistically significant difference between the efficiency and performance of public and private operators'.[*] The good performance of public water utilities in cities such as Phnom Penh and Penang by far outshines the record of private suppliers in others, including Jakarta and Manila. And in Germany, the small-scale distribution network of Bavaria is economically more efficient than the more large-scale operations in the neighbouring *Land*, Baden-Württemberg.

On a global scale, about 90 per cent of all water is still supplied by public utilities. About half of the world's 400 biggest cities have attempted to privatise their drinking water supply systems – with negative consequences in nearly all cases. Today, 88 per cent of the big cities continue to rely on or have reintroduced public supply systems. The trend of the last few years is that the global water corporations only want to invest if sufficient profits can be secured in a relatively short term.

---

[*] A. Estache, S. Perelman and L. Trujillo (2005) 'Infrastructure Performance and Reform in Developing and Transition Economies: Evidence from a Survey of Productivity Measures', *Policy Research Working Paper 3514*, World Bank, Washington.

The failure of water privatisation is hard to swallow in neoliberal policy elite circles. One reaction has been a marked reticence of financial service providers when it comes to providing credit finance for the modernisation of public water supply systems. Political, financial and other hurdles prevent public water delivery from achieving its full potential. The question today therefore is not *whether* public water supply works – it does – but *how* it works.

## Negative Examples of Privatisation

A series of cases illustrate that concerns over water privatisation voiced by trade unions and environmentalist organisations were indeed well-founded.

### United Kingdom

'Raid', 'legalised robbery', 'swindle' and 'piracy' – even the *Financial Times* used these terms when commenting on the British water privatisation in 1995.* And the *Daily Mail* (11 July 1994) called it 'the biggest licensed robbery in the history of England'.

Up to 1973, water supply and wastewater disposal were in the hands of many different communal and private operators. The systems were reliable and conformed to health standards. Water prices were set with customers' ability to pay in mind, rather than cost-effectiveness, and were publicly subsidised. The profits of private operators, which made up about 20 per cent of the sector, were subject to a legally fixed maximum of 5 per cent.

In 1973, responsibility for water supply matters was taken away from the communities and handed over to ten regional water authorities with a view to later privatisation. In the lead-up to privatisation in 1989, the workforce was reduced by half, from some 80,000 to slightly more than 40,000 employees. To ensure favourable starting conditions for the newly

---

* Richard Freeman, writing in the *Financial Times* (1996) as quoted in Salim J. Loxley, *An Analysis of a Public–Private Sector Partnership: The Hamilton–Wentworth–Philips Utilities Management Corporation PPP*, Manitoba, 1999.

privatised water utilities, the government cancelled existing debts and granted generous tax exemptions to promote investment. In addition, significant rate increases were approved. The private suppliers had to agree to serve everyone within their allotted territory; in return, they received a 25-year licence protecting them against any competition in this territory – that is, privatisation without competition.

After privatisation, job slashing and outsourcing continued. Water prices kept rising, and so did the incomes of top-echelon managers – up to 570 per cent during the first four years alone. Approval for further price hikes was sought and granted, as the utilities said they would invest additional revenue. However, the promised investments often failed to materialise, and as a result, the nationwide share of low-quality drinking water has grown to 11 per cent. Up to 25 per cent of all water fed into the system is lost through leaks in the transport pipes. As a result of this entrepreneurial policy, the companies' profits doubled during the first ten years following privatisation, exceeding £2 billion per year, while low-income households found paying their water bill increasingly difficult. In 1994, more than 15 per cent of households were in arrears with their water bills. The water companies responded by introducing upfront payment schemes and automatic discontinuation of service in case of non-payment. The introduction of a regulatory system from the mid-1990s finally curbed the worst excesses of corporate greed.

## El Alto (Bolivia)

After the World Bank had made the privatisation of communal water utilities a condition for debt relief in the mid-1990s, the water supply systems of Bolivia's capital, La Paz, and of the city of El Alto (approximately 700,000 inhabitants) were privatised. A subsidiary of the Suez group was granted a 30-year licence in 1997. Investments of US$68 million were planned to connect 70,000 households to the drinking water supply network during the first five years of operation. This target was never reached – but water prices were heavily increased between 1997 and 2001. When the rates were finally 'dollarised' in 2001, prices soared by an additional 120 per cent, causing violent protests and the eventual failure of the contract.

## Cochabamba (Bolivia)

Two years after the conclusion of the El Alto deal, the water works of Bolivia's third-largest city, Cochabamba (approximately 800,000 inhabitants), were up for sale in 1999. Under the terms of the agreement, no upfront purchase price had to be paid; rather, the private operator, a subsidiary of the US group Bechtel, would have to start payments when revenue began to come in, subject to a guaranteed 15 per cent yield for the company. The deal was to be funded via price increases that would promote more efficient water use, or so it was argued. Water and sewage disposal rates soared to nine times the previous levels, or about one third of the average worker's wages. The city's inhabitants responded with massive protests that finally led to the cancellation of the supply contract.

The re-communalisation of water supply systems triggered a process of democratisation that involved representatives of the people in planning and decision-making. Meanwhile, Bolivia's new Minister for Water Management, Abel Mamani, has presented a strategy for the reversal of water privatisations in his country. Mamani was a leader of the Bolivian protest movement against the French water supply group Suez in El Alto.

## Tucumán (Argentina)

When the Suez group took over the water supply and wastewater disposal systems in the province of Tucumán in 1993 and raised the rates by more than 100 per cent, the inhabitants of the province responded with civil disobedience and founded a consumer advocacy association. After germs had been found in tap water, the organised citizens of the province refused to pay their water bills. The government of the province that instituted legal proceedings against Suez took up the matter. The group at first threatened to stop supplies, and when that threat did not work, tried to negotiate new contract terms. Eventually, Suez pulled out of the region, refused to meet its contractual obligations and took its case against the consumers to the International Centre for Settlement of Investment Disputes (a sub-organisation of the World Bank). The arbitrators, however, decided in favour of the province of Tucumán.

In September 2005 it became clear that the Argentinian government was not going to accept any more requests for water rate increases from private companies.

## Tallinn (Estonia)

In 2001, the Estonian capital sold a 50.4 per cent stake in its economically efficient utility Tallinna Vesi to British industrial investors. Before the deal, the company had been successfully modernised in cooperation with the communally owned Stockholm Water utility. Only a few months after the sale, which earned the city of Tallinn proceeds of €40 million, the water utility began paying out handsome dividends to its new owners. Steps were taken to further increase revenue, including a reduction of equity cover, billing the city for drainage services, and a 15 per cent water price hike. Moreover, the company workforce was reduced by 40 per cent within two years. With this strategy, the new owners were able to recover most of the purchase price within only four years. For the people of Tallinn, the effects were higher water prices and unemployment rates.

## Potsdam (Germany)

The city of Potsdam concluded an operating agreement with the company Eurawasser (a joint venture of Suez Lyonnaise des Eaux and Thyssen-Krupp) in 1997 under which Eurawasser was to provide water treatment and wastewater disposal services in return for a 49 per cent stake in the city's water works. This attempt at partial privatisation ended abruptly in 2000. According to the city, the planned increase in rates was not acceptable.

### Atlanta (USA)

In the USA, water has for the last century been provided as a public service at the taxpayers' expense. But there have also been trends towards privatisation.

In January 2003, the city of Atlanta decided to terminate all water contracts with the Suez group and reverse the privatisation move of 1999. In addition to drastic price increases and lack of new investments, declining water quality, reduction of the workforce by half and fraudulent billing resulting in excessive debts were cited as reasons for this step.

Meanwhile, another segment of the water business is on the rise in the US: bottled water. Bottled water sold by private companies costs up to 10,000 times as much as public tap water, even if it comes from the same original source. Today, bottled water ranks second in sales among commercial beverages in the US, with sales exceeding US$22 billion annually. Transnational food corporations such as Nestlé, Danone, Coca-Cola and Pepsi dominate the industry.

### Manila (Philippines)

With some 12 million inhabitants, Manila is one of the fastest-growing urban conglomerates of Southeast Asia. In the mid-1990s, one third of inhabitants did not have running water in their homes, and there was only a rudimentary sewage system. Old pipelines and the widespread practice of illegal tapping of the system led to massive water losses and low revenues of the communal supply system. The World Bank and the Asian Development Bank (ADB) called for privatisation. Following an international tender, two private operators received 25-year operating licences for the distribution network in 1996: one for Manila's east, one for the western part of the city. One of the companies is owned by the Filipino Lopez family and the French Suez group, the other by the Ayala family and the US construction group Bechtel. Promises were made that water would be supplied to everyone within ten years, that system losses would be halved and that prices would remain stable.

By 2001, not only had the two operating companies failed to reduce water losses, but losses had even jumped to more than 70 per cent in the western part of Manila. Investments in new infrastructure lagged behind, reaching only 50–70 per cent of what had been promised. On the other hand, 46 new top managers were hired at handsome salaries. When the situation did not improve even after a number of substantial price increases, the first of the two licensing agreements was terminated in 2002.

## Public Water Services – Good Practice Examples

### Phnom Penh (Cambodia)

A communal authority manages the water supply of Cambodia's capital Phnom Penh. In 1993, only 20 per cent of the city's inhabitants were connected to the distribution network, while 70 per cent of the water was illegally siphoned off. The pipelines were obsolete to the point of breakdown, and the water authority was plagued by corruption and inefficiency. However, it managed to successfully reorganise the system within ten years, installing over 750 km of new water mains, repairing the existing 250 km of pipelines, and connecting 85 per cent of the inhabitants (nearly 100 per cent in the core urban areas) to the distribution network. Nearly all new connections have water meters. The price is US$0.50 per cubic metre, much less than what the poor formerly had to pay to private water traders. Good-quality water is now available 24 hours a day. Japanese investors wanted to buy an interest in the system in 2003, but their offer was rejected by the city. In 2004, the city of Phnom Penh received an award of excellence from the ADB for its water supply system, by now one of the best on the continent.

### Penang (Malaysia)

The public water utility in the city of Penang delivers water to 100 per cent of the population. It combines commercial outlook with social obligations.

Due to the very low levels of non-revenue water (leakages), tariffs are affordable for all citizens. Part of the success is a strong public service ethos and a commitment to serve the population by the management and the workers, who own part of the shares in the company. For the rest, the utility is publicly owned but administratively independent. This prevents problematic political interference while enabling the population to hold the company accountable.

## Porto Alegre (Brazil)

Although Porto Alegre, one of Brazil's big cities, grew dynamically throughout the 1990s, the municipal water utility was able to improve water supply to households substantially. The proportion of households connected to the water distribution network was raised from 95 per cent to 99.5 per cent, that of sewer system connections from 70 per cent to 84 per cent. This development was decisively stimulated by the city's inhabitants through participation in the city's budget planning processes (Participatory Budget). The resulting policies have been atypical for Brazil in that they did not benefit an influential clientele, but aimed at investment in low-income areas of the city. The extraordinary success of civil society participation in urban development planning stands out internationally as an example of good practice. An independent deliberative council controls the public utility and has a say in investment decisions and pricing. Water quality in Porto Alegre is good, and water prices are low compared to other parts of Brazil. Additionally, discounts are granted to the lowest-income households.

## South America

Democratic water management in Brazil is also to be found in Recife, Caxias do Sul, Santo Andre and Jacaré and Piracicaba. And the biggest utility worldwide, SABESP in São Paulo, was able to improve its efficiency through an extensive modernisation programme that was carried out in cooperation with the trade unions: operating costs were cut by half, water supply and sewerage systems were expanded.

In Venezuela, a model of far-reaching user engagement in water management has been under development since 1999. Almost all public water operators in the country have adopted this model of participatory planning and management. The national coverage of drinking water increased from 81 per cent in 1998 to 89 per cent in 2003.

## Hope for the Future

In the wake of many negative water privatisation outcomes, the advocates of privatisation have changed their line of argument. The focus has shifted from privatisation as such to the financial power of private investors. Investments of US$180 billion annually are necessary, privatisation advocates claim, to achieve the Johannesburg World Summit on Social Development goal (halving the number of people without access to clean water by 2015) – an amount which the public budgets of developing countries will not be able to provide; thus, it is argued, private investment will be needed. However, there are also serious estimates that put the required investment volume at no more than US$10 billion annually. This could be raised by increases in development aid, debt relief and reprioritising of government budgets.

There is already worldwide resistance against the water business. The advocates of water as a human right have formed a global coalition under the name Blue Planet Project that includes activists from environmentalist groups and trade unions, and from developed and developing countries. More and more big corporations are withdrawing from the global water business. The Suez group announced in 2003 that it would withdraw from the poor countries, and RWE announced the sale of Thames Water and American Waterworks in 2005. Even World Bank Vice President Katherine Sierra admitted at the 2005 Water Week in Washington that the World Bank's exclusive support for the private sector during the 1990s was ideologically motivated. Appeals were made for more government support for communal water administrations and development projects at the Fourth World Water Forum in Mexico City in 2006.

South Africa included the right to water in its constitution in 1997, and Uruguay did the same in 2005. The city of Vienna added a provision protecting its water supply system against privatisation to its municipal constitution in 2001. The UN Committee on Economic, Social and Cultural Rights adopted a General Comment in 2002 which declares a 'human right to water' that 'entitles everyone to sufficient, safe, acceptable, physically accessible and affordable water for personal and domestic uses'.[*] The next and decisive step will be a UN convention on the right to water.

Trade unions also have to struggle for the human right to water. The union movement has many partners in civil society regarding this issue. The water supply example clearly shows that privatisation brings disadvantages for ordinary people. Privatisation means rising water prices and the deterioration of supply systems. While employees lose their jobs, managers and new owners get rich.

---

[*] 'Substantive Issues Arising in the Implementation of the International Covenant on Economic, Social and Cultural Rights: General Comment No. 15 (2002) – The Right to Water (arts. 11 and 12 of the International Covenant on Economic, Social and Cultural Rights.'

# 11

# Solid Waste Management

'Waste will always look for the cheapest hole', as an old maxim of waste management wisdom has it. In times of globalisation and liberalisation, this means that waste is transported and traded, for example from southern Italy, where overflowing landfills have been closed down, to Germany, where too many incinerators were built in the 1990s at the taxpayers' expense – the operators have turned to waste imports to fill the excess capacities.

But globalisation also means that electronic trash from Western countries, camouflaged as serviceable second-hand equipment, or even labelled 'development aid', is exported to the so-called Third World. Lagos, the largest city in Nigeria, alone receives some 500 containers filled with worn-out computers and screens every month. The trash shipments are incinerated there, poisoning people and the environment. The alleged 'recycling companies' in Europe or the United States that are paid for accepting the trash thus save themselves the expense of proper disposal.

## Historical Development

### Europe: Progress Through Early Communalisation

Waste disposal has not always been a profitable business. Although four high-ranking officials (aediles) were responsible for street cleaning in ancient Rome, the usual practice was simply to wash dirt from the street surface down into the sewers. Residents had to take care of waste disposal themselves, which often took the form of throwing domestic waste from windows or balconies. There was no regular litter collection system.

The history of urban solid waste management in Europe begins in the fifteenth century. When it was no longer deemed acceptable to get rid of household and commercial waste and even human excrement by simply throwing it out on the street or into waterways, waste was for the first time collected, to be deposited on fields outside town. The waste collectors were usually farmers from the environs of the towns who collected horse manure, ashes and other biological waste materials to use them as fertiliser on their fields. Obviously, these early waste removal operations left much to be desired and were frequently late in meeting their disposal duties.

Thus, waste was increasingly seen as a sanitary and social problem. Communal garbage collection operations were first introduced in the second half of the nineteenth century, and by the early twentieth century most cities ran such operations. More time – in some cases decades – elapsed before the waste collection systems reached the necessary technical standard to provide full and functioning service to all parts of an urban community. Only at a relatively late point did waste management benefit from the technological advances made in the water, gas and electricity sectors. For a long time, waste was simply dumped outside the cities. The only exception was Britain, where waste incineration was introduced around 1870. By 1900, more than 120 incinerators operated there, whereas incineration was only just being introduced on the continent. The first German waste incinerator was built in Hamburg in 1894. Waste removal in covered containers and the first attempts at sorting garbage also date back to the period before the First World War.

## Waste Disposal at the Start of the New Millennium

### Global Differences in the Quality of Waste Disposal Systems

Different levels of national development affect waste management practices. Some countries have comprehensive, top-standard public waste management systems (garbage collection, sorting schemes, recycling), strict legislation and functioning controls. Investment in infrastructure is high, as is public awareness concerning waste prevention and at-source separation. This group includes the countries of Western and Northern Europe, Canada, Australia, New Zealand, Japan, Korea and Singapore.

Another group of states have more or less working waste disposal systems, but legislation – or its implementation – still leaves a lot to be desired. Infrastructure tends to be obsolete, and there is little awareness concerning waste prevention and at-source separation of waste materials. This group includes, at various levels, most countries of Eastern and Southern Europe and many newly developed countries.

Finally, there are countries where public waste disposal systems are insufficient or work poorly. This group includes practically all of the so-called developing countries and in particular the big cities in these countries. Traditionally, much is left to private initiative there.

## Different Forms of Organisation

Waste disposal is regarded as a service of public interest in most developed countries. Local communities are most often responsible for waste management, and they either buy in services from private contractors or run their own public systems, alone or in collaboration with other communities. In some cases, whole segments of the waste management system are contracted out, such as the profitable collection and recycling of scrap metal, waste paper and glass.

The private sector share in waste management varies across Europe. While garbage collection is a public service in most countries, further waste treatment is largely privatised in a number of them. The two biggest European companies in the sector are both headquartered in France: Sita, the waste division of Suez, employs a workforce of over 45,000; Onyx, the waste division of Veolia, has more than 70,000 employees on its payroll. The third rank is occupied by Remondis, a German company.

Privatisation has progressed most markedly in the United States, where more than 50 per cent of communities have contracted out waste management services, either in part or as a whole. It must be noted, however, that 20 years ago, private waste management operators already had a share of some 30 per cent. Obviously, private sector shares are highest in services that are profitable.

Many developing or newly developed countries, including Indonesia, Malaysia, Singapore and Thailand, also rely increasingly on private companies for waste management functions. Singapore has privatised all waste collection and incineration/landfill activities. And Malaysia has invited private companies to apply for waste licences under a public–private partnership scheme. Local communities in the region spend a large portion of their budgets on waste management – in Malaysia, a full 50 per cent, of which 70 per cent go towards waste collection. Some cities in the region, notably Bangkok, Singapore and Jakarta, have introduced deposits on certain types of packaging to support recycling efforts. For other types of packaging, waste disposal charges are added to the price of the package.

Most big cities in southern and western Asia lack the financial resources that would be needed to set up functioning waste management systems. There is no money for necessary investments in improved collection, transport and disposal schemes. Waste treatment continues to be one of the most pressing urban problems in the region.

Beginning in the 1970s, state and regional subsidies have repeatedly been paid to major cities in India to help improve their urban infrastructures. In general, the communities have to rely on their own tax revenues, most of which come from property taxes. Waste disposal charges are largely non-existent, the only exception being major businesses and big hotels that sometimes pay for disposal services (provided by communal or private waste collectors). But the majority of low-income city-dwellers cannot pay any charges so that there are no or next to no waste disposal services in their neighbourhoods. Those living along the street often pay the street cleaners in Indian cities. Garbage collection has been fully privatised in several large cities (Delhi, Madras, Ahmadabad, Baroda, Bangalore and Rajkot), and Delhi has also conducted a tender for the construction of a landfill. Despite these privatisation measures, the number of employees has not been reduced in many cases due to strong union opposition.

The situation is much more dramatic in Pakistan, where only some 50–70 per cent of household waste is collected. The number of legal disposal facilities that could be expanded is too small, and due to a lack of public awareness and education, most waste is deposited just anywhere. Communal street-cleaning services are unreliable and usually restricted to main roads. The layout of cities poses additional problems, as large tracts of land are covered by sprawling settlements intersected by narrow lanes that are often hardly passable for vehicles. Garbage collection vans are regularly out of service or are misused for other purposes. A large share of all work is done manually. Reusable and recyclable materials (paper, plastic, glass, metal) are removed by private collectors at no cost or against payment of small fees. Industrial and hazardous wastes pose a particularly grave problem, as there is no separate collection of these wastes, and they are mostly burned in open fires.

In Kenya, existing private waste collection and disposal operations usually work better than public ones. The government of Egypt decided in May 2000 to privatise waste management with the help of the German Deutsche Gesellschaft für Technische Zusammenarbeit (GTZ) GmbH to solve the problem of highly inefficient waste management systems that were unable to cover operating costs. Egyptian communities are faced with growing waste volumes that have already created serious health and environmental problems in many parts of the country. Existing disposal schemes and capacities are unable to cope with the amount of waste generated.

## Advantages and Drawbacks of Privatisation

The above-cited examples illustrate that private companies may indeed contribute to the development of effective waste management systems in the countries of the so-called Third World – provided that a suitable legal and political framework is in place and that the poorer population segments are also in a position to benefit.

Having said that, it must be noted that high environmental quality is attained in countries such as Germany and Austria precisely because of communal responsibility for sewage systems and waste management. In addition to environmentally sound practices, the system users benefit from consumer protection and socially acceptable price rates. These achievements are due to the fact that local inhabitants are the ones who call for environmental quality, and local public utilities are the organisations charged with meeting the people's demands directly and at affordable prices.

The drawbacks of complete privatisation are obvious: loss of local influence, no direct access to waste-relevant data, loss of cost control (externalisation of factors), loss of fairness in pricing, definition of quality standards in terms of business goals instead of national economic considerations, and decline of environmental standards to legal minimum levels. But when problems arise, people still turn to the communal administration for solutions. Minor efficiency gains on one side are outweighed by a growing need for (and the cost of) monitoring and control, regulation and public guarantees.

Privatisation does not ensure more competition. The waste management industry is currently going through a massive consolidation and concentration process that only a handful of international corporations will survive in the long run. As companies seek to take over competitors or push them out of business, social standards are undercut, and workers and consumers' rights are eroded. Progressive market consolidation leads to less competition instead of more; 'gentlemen's agreements' and cartels drive up prices. Thus, a relentless policy of ever 'more market and competition' is bound to result in an oligopoly of only a few big corporations.

Communities are at a disadvantage in this competition among other things because they are rarely allowed to provide services outside their own territory – a constraint that does not apply to private players. And they are supposed to set good-practice examples as employers and protectors of the environment – a role which private companies do not have to play.

More competition drives up waste generation. Because competing private companies must work to expand their markets and maximise their profits, privatised waste management operators are not likely to educate customers to reduce waste generation. Critical consumer behaviour, environmentally sound handling of products and wastes by customers and at-source waste reduction are, after all, harmful to the business results of the waste management operations.

As elsewhere, privatisation in the waste management sector leads to wage cuts and social dumping. In Europe, privatised services have reduced the number of jobs (early retirement, redundancies, and so on), taken in fewer apprentices, and reduced employees' incomes (cuts in wage supplements and social benefits). New market entrants undercut existing wage levels and employment standards (part-time jobs, temporary work). As a result, working conditions deteriorate (increased work intensity, loss of job security), and the provisions of collective agreements are frequently disregarded. In Germany, a number of local politicians are no longer prepared to accept the wage dumping that is a result of privatisation. Three local governments in the state of Brandenburg have already decided not to extend contracts with private operators, but to re-communalise waste management.

## Conclusions

The privatisation of waste management operations in developed countries has frequently led to negative outcomes in terms of the quality and price of service. Other negative effects concern the scope and effectiveness of democratic controls, accountability of operators (especially if they are transnational corporations), employment and working conditions. In general, the role of the market in waste management must be limited because privatisation, cut-throat competition and monopolistic market concentration make it more difficult to control the generation, collection, removal and disposal of waste.

Communal management organisations and local public services fulfil functions that are essential for the well-being of everyone. Defining 'free competition' as the single most important priority is to sacrifice these essential functions. This must not happen. Specifically, where businesses' interests in the free movement of goods clash with ecological considerations, the latter must prevail. What is at stake is the protection of human health and of the environment against potential threats.

Good waste management policy defines waste prevention as its top priority, followed by recycling; that is, the recovery and reuse of valuable materials – incidentally also an activity with significant job potential. Where waste can neither be reduced nor recycled, low-impact disposal technologies should be considered, such as waste incineration with thermal energy recovery.

Moreover, communal waste management should ensure fair prices; that is, affordable, socially acceptable rates for everyone, and should act in a socially responsible way as an employer.

The primary task of the trade unions in this context is to fight for the introduction and continued existence of high social standards in the waste management industry. Waste management operations must be made to comply with regulatory provisions concerning working conditions, and to honour collective wage agreements. In this context, it is important to establish cross-border works councils in international waste management corporations.

# 12

# Gas and Electricity

The influence of efficient energy systems on a country's economic and industrial development in particular cannot be overestimated. It was the main reason why, in the late nineteenth and early twentieth centuries, states decided to make energy supply their own responsibility.

## Historical Development

Basically, it was only the nineteenth and the early twentieth centuries that witnessed a technological breakthrough and the advent of modern types of energy such as steam, electricity, gas and oil. In the industrialised regions and states of the world, traditional energy sources, such as wood, coal and the horse, were increasingly replaced.

In 1807, the first gas lamps for street lighting were put into operation in London. From the 1820s on, many European cities followed London's example. The lamps were lit by so-called 'town gas', which was produced through gasification of coal. The first German gas works for the production of town gas was established in Hanover in 1825. Gas lighting superseded oil lamps, which had characterised the streetscape for some 150 years. The bright and even light provided by gas also made it possible to introduce night shifts, for example in the textile industry.

In the 1850s many cities commissioned private companies to develop their gas supply and licences were granted for 30 or 40 years. Thus, between 1885 and 1890, many towns and cities faced the question of either extending the existing licences or buying out and operating the gas companies themselves.

The experience gained until that time clearly spoke against a solution favouring the private sector. The licence provisions regarding security of supply, tariff policy and maximum yield, which were agreed upon to safeguard the public interest, had very often not fulfilled their purpose.

At the same time, this situation had an impact on the electrification of towns and cities, which was beginning at about the same time. In the 1880s, private electricity companies were founded throughout Europe, and it was anticipated that these would achieve the same good commercial results as had been the case with gas. In view of the experience they had gained, municipal authorities, however, allowed only pilot companies to provide electrical street lighting. At the time the decision had not yet been made as to whether electricity or gas was the more suitable solution. As the gas companies were facing the threat of street lighting being electrified, and in view of the poor prospects for business, they became less reluctant to accept the possibility of municipal buyout.

Indeed, gas lighting using town gas remained common in Europe until the 1970s, and many historic town centres remain gas-lit to this very day. In Vienna, the change from town gas to natural gas was completed only in 1978, and its use continued in Berlin into the 1990s. An alternative to town gas – natural gas – had been commercially used as early as 1821 in Fredonia (USA), but it was only in the 1940s and 1950s that the large-scale development of natural gas supply and transmission began in the USA. Liquid natural gas was transported by ship to Britain for the first time in 1959. From the mid-1960s onwards, when large natural gas resources were discovered in the North Sea, town gas was gradually displaced by natural gas across the European continent.

Generally speaking, the proportion of electricity production capacities under public control was initially rather low. However, around 1900, many European towns and cities started to establish their own municipal power companies, or they bought up private companies whose initial licences had expired. In Switzerland, the proportion of municipal power supply in public ownership was less than 15 per cent around 1900. By 1920 this share had already reached one third, and by around 1950 it had risen to 56 per cent. The Swiss canton of Zurich, for instance, founded its own electricity company as early as 1908. The liberal newspaper *Neue Zürcher Zeitung* perceived its creation as a positive sign, and accordingly affirmed that provision of a publicly administered power supply for the canton was a key task of the state.

Thus, at the beginning of the twentieth century there was basic consensus on the importance and necessity of ensuring that energy provision and supply was a municipal task. The necessity for long-term planning and coordination was a major reason why many governments in many countries of the world took control of their power sector during the first half of the twentieth century.

The First World War led to a strong increase in goods production in the processing industry. Concurrent with the requirements of the arms industry, the demand for energy production rose quickly, and security of supply also had to be improved. During the reconstruction period following the First World War, industrial production continued to grow at a rapid pace. The use of electricity was no longer restricted to lighting, but now encompassed machinery and equipment, cranes, means of public transport and household appliances. The Soviet Union even went so far as to announce that communism was Soviet power plus the electrification of the whole country. Large power plants were constructed and high-voltage transmission networks installed. The electrification of rural areas, particularly for the needs of agriculture, also pushed ahead.

During the Second World War, power plants and supply networks became preferred targets for air raids. After the war, Europe was characterised by an enormous electricity shortage. Network instability, sudden voltage drops and power failures were the order of the day. The most important goal was to guarantee security of supply. For this reason a number of countries, including Britain and France, decided to nationalise the energy sector. Gaz de France was founded in 1946, and Électricité de France was established in 1948. In Britain, more than a thousand private and municipal gas companies were transferred to twelve regional authorities, as the nation's power generation and distribution had been nationalised as early as 1926.

Until the 1970s, public ownership of the energy sector remained undisputed. The obvious economic argument was safe energy supply at moderate prices. The prices for the supply of energy were not commodity prices but tariffs, which were relatively independent of costs and profits of energy production and rather depended on the strategic significance of the energy customer for the economy as a whole. The security aspect was another argument in favour of public ownership. Since the nineteenth century, coal production had been part of the mining sector that also served armament purposes. The nuclear energy sector has received public funds since the middle of the twentieth century on account of its 'dual use' technology concept. The safeguarding of oil reserves may even lead to wars, as has recently been the case in Iraq.

## Privatisation of Energy Supply Since the 1970s

From the 1970s on, the situation changed. During the 1980s the need for planning and maintenance began to become subsidiary to the desire to commercialise power provision. And during the 1990s, electricity was liberalised, privatised and deregulated around the world. The procedure was for the most part the same: a discrediting of the state monopoly, and, in the event of more competition, the promise of a better supply at lower prices, the privatisation of energy companies, reduction in costs, the downsizing of workforces, and an increase in energy prices and profits. There were no advantages; indeed, there were often disadvantages for the consumers arising from higher prices and reduced security of supply.

The private energy sector began to organise itself transnationally as early as 1924. The World Energy Council (WEC) has remained an influential think tank to this very day. Its members are the world's largest energy groups as well as consultancy companies in the energy sector. The WEC commissions research on questions pertaining to the energy industry and energy policy, and issues policy recommendations.

The International Energy Agency (IEA) also lobbies for the liberalisation and deregulation of energy markets. It was founded in 1973 by industrial nations to coordinate their response to the oil crisis, and in 1974 became part of the OECD. The IEA strives for a worldwide reduction in energy sector trade barriers as well as a legal framework for the protection of private investments as represented by GATS – the General Agreement on Trade in Services of the World Trade Organisation (WTO). To achieve these aims, IEA closely cooperates with the International Monetary Fund (IMF) and the World Bank.

Chile was the first country to launch a drastic privatisation programme following the military coup of 1973. Subsequently, energy prices reached record levels, with a number of senior officials of the military junta consequently becoming rich. Between 1974 and 1986, the number of employees in state enterprises declined by 40 per cent. Brazil's power generation was auctioned off in 1996. Consumers experienced massive price rises, while the new foreign owners repatriated their profits and avoided investment in new generating capacity.

## United Kingdom

After Margaret Thatcher's accession to power in 1979, many public services were privatised, among them gas and power. British Gas, which had been created in 1949, was privatised in 1986. The enterprise was sold in its entirety because the price obtained in the capital market was considerably higher for a monopoly than for an enterprise facing competition. However, in 1995, British Gas was split up in order to create competition in the marketplace. By that time British Gas had been engaged in a persistent and successful fight to maintain its private monopoly status. In order to maintain its market share, the company exercised its control over the pipe network, the gas distribution infrastructure and its almost exclusive access to North Sea gas production. The newly established regulatory authority, Ofgas, failed to significantly alter this situation. Despite liberalisation measures during the 1990s, only 10 per cent of Britain's gas supply came from alternative suppliers.

Britain's electricity supply had been nationalised by the Labour Party in 1926. The objective was to standardise the power frequency and voltage used as well as to reclassify the smallest supply areas. In 1990, the power industry was subdivided into several companies and privatised. Fossil-fuelled power plants, nuclear power plants and the transmission network were transferred to separate companies. All electricity suppliers were provided with access to the grid via an electricity 'pool'. In reality, only about 10 per cent of the electricity supplied was traded at pool prices. Individual major customers were offered long-term supply contracts with fixed prices and fixed purchase quantities.

Since 1989, the number of people working in the electricity sector has dropped dramatically – by some 70 per cent, in fact. This has resulted in considerable increases in efficiency. Nonetheless, electricity costs clearly remained above actual production costs, which resulted in tidy and mounting profits for the private shareholders. It was only by market regulation and the supervision by the regulatory authority, Ofgem, that some of the cost benefits were passed on to the consumer in the form of price reductions.

## California

As in Europe, in the USA, too, energy supply to a certain area for a long time was regarded as a natural monopoly. This involved a supply duty vis-à-vis the customer and tariffs regulated with costs in mind. The legal basis for all of this was the 1935 Federal Power Act. According to this act, public utility commissions at state level monitored compliance with the end-user market regulations.

In 1992, a federal act liberalised the US wholesale energy market, while the states remained responsible for the regulation of the end-user services. California decided to fully open its end-user market in 1998. An independent system operator and an electricity exchange were established. The private suppliers were obliged to obtain all their power through the exchange and all production was to be sold to the same.

Liberalisation started at a time when no surplus capacities were available, as prospective new power plant developments were examined strictly on the basis of necessity. However, demand had been assessed at too low a level, and capacities had not been substantially expanded prior to liberalisation. Moreover, the existing power stations were partially obsolete and there was increased risk of failure. Private investors, on the other hand, had no reason to invest in constructing new plants. To top it all off, instead of carrying out urgently needed repair works, up to 25 per cent of plant capacity was closed down.

In the course of 1999 there were already a number of isolated short-term power bottlenecks and strong price hikes. The situation became even more aggravated in 2000. In December 2000, available production reserves had decreased so much that several blackouts occurred. Within a year the price of electrical energy on the exchange had risen fifty-fold. As the suppliers could not pass on these enormous price increases to their private consumers, the three largest companies were forced to declare themselves insolvent. The electricity exchange itself also filed for bankruptcy. In 2001, the State of California intervened and signed supply contracts with power suppliers at prices that were, however, astronomical. These agreements remain in force. Although California filed complaints and repayment claims with the courts against private suppliers who had deliberately caused an electricity shortage, most losses incurred by the Californian power disaster have been borne by the state and thus the public, no matter what the outcome of the proceedings will be.

California may be the most publicised example of price manipulation, but there are many others in the US. Since federal deregulation of wholesale electricity prices in 1996, prices doubled and quadrupled. Those US states that have not deregulated their power markets have not experienced these large increases. In the USA, deregulation has also led to a massive reduction in the utility labour force, with 150,000 people losing their jobs, while at the same time a lack of maintenance contributed to the blackouts.

### Argentina

Since 1989, under the government of Carlos Menem, numerous Argentine enterprises were privatised; among them was the power industry. The Dirección General de Agua y Energía Eléctrica had been responsible for electricity supply across large parts of Argentina since 1947. As is customary in Latin America, the power sector was split into energy production, transmission and distribution sectors. In order to make those divisions that were to be privatised as attractive as possible to buyers, employees were subjected to 'voluntary early retirement schemes'. During the 1992 privatisation, companies were mostly sold to foreign buyers. To reduce the trade unions' resistance to privatisation, an employee participation programme was introduced in 1994. Depending on the enterprise, employees could acquire between 2 per cent and 12 per cent of the total shares under favourable conditions. Similar tactics were employed in almost all privatisation processes in Latin America, and they were also successful in the case of Argentina.

Nevertheless, this drastic privatisation destroyed the country's economic structures. From 1999 on, Argentina experienced a dramatic economic crisis from which the country has not fully recovered. In the aftermath of the crisis the government no longer tied the currency to the US dollar and froze energy prices. For this reason some foreign investors left the country, while others took the government to the courts. Enterprises have been trying to reduce costs ever since through the introduction of less favourable working conditions, outsourcing and temporary work contracts as well as increases in the length of the working week.

## Senegal

As in many other African states, after gaining independence in 1960, the public economic sector played a key role in Senegal's economic and social development. The state had to satisfy the basic needs of the population, and actually managed to do so quite successfully in the 1960s and 1970s, thanks to the performance of the agricultural sector. Senegal also achieved significant improvements in the spheres of health and education.

The economic recession started in the mid-1970s after a number of droughts. Agricultural exports declined, foreign indebtedness soared, and the Senegalese government had to ask the IMF and the World Bank for help. Within the framework of its Stabilisation Programme and Structural Adjustment Programme, Senegal was instructed to cut public expenditure, reduce the influence of the public sector and privatise state-owned enterprises and services of general interest. The consequence was the dissolution of state-related enterprises and the collapse of the agricultural and industrial sectors as a result of cheap imports from developed countries, which increased considerably as a result of opening up the market.

Instructions to privatise also encompassed the state-owned electricity company SENELEC, a measure that was opposed by both the government and the trade unions. In 1998, one third of the shares were sold to the French-Canadian group EHQ (Elyo Hydro-Quebec). However, the promised investments were not made, and power outages occurred repeatedly. This led to a decrease in the entire economic performance and numerous job losses, followed by unrest and the ousting of the government in 2000. Pressured by the trade unions, the new government decided to reverse the privatisation policy. The World Bank conceded that the privatisation of SENELEC had led to enormous financial, social and long-term economic costs for the state. Nevertheless, it 'encouraged' the new government to engage in new privatisation adventures.

For now, however, SENELEC remains a public enterprise, and has clearly improved its economic performance since 2001. In 2004, a small profit was generated for the first time, and there are 50 per cent fewer power outages than there were in 2000.


## Thailand

By the end of the 1990s, Thailand was suffering from the aftermath of the economic and financial crisis that had hit the whole of Southeast Asia. The IMF was prepared to grant a reorganisation loan provided there was an acceleration of the privatisation of public enterprises. More than half of the 63 state-owned enterprises were to be privatised, including the energy sector.

Thaksin Shinawatra, Thailand's wealthiest businessman, became Prime Minister in 2001. He pressed ahead with a privatisation campaign, with himself and his extended family benefiting from these efforts. However, in 2004 there was strong resistance against the privatisation of the energy and water sectors by the trade unions, which also gained international support, especially from PSI and its affiliates. This protest turned into a general anti-privatisation campaign. Finally, the government gave in and withdrew the privatisation plan. When Thaksin won the parliamentary elections in 2005, he again tried to embark on privatisation. A decision by the Supreme Administrative Court ruled that the short-term privatisation programme should be rescinded. In the meantime he was forced to resign, and the 2005 elections were declared null and void.

## Bolivia

Even though it has the second largest natural gas resources in South America – 90 per cent of which are exported, predominantly to Argentina and Brazil – Bolivia is the poorest country in Latin America.

Until a short time ago, the population of Bolivia did not benefit much from the country's mineral wealth. In 1994, foreign investors were granted the most generous terms regarding the exploitation of resources. Indeed, the taxes they had to pay the state amounted to only 18 per cent of their revenues. The handling of the gas reserves had been a hot topic for years, leading to widespread protests in 2003. In a referendum, the majority of the population voted for a nationalisation of gas and oil reserves. These demands were the reason for Evo Morales' victory in the presidential elections held in December 2005. On 1 May 2006, Morales put into practice the promises made in the election campaign. The state took control over gas production, handled its distribution and fixed domestic and export prices. Henceforth, foreign investors can only become engaged in joint ventures with the Bolivian state; moreover, they are subject to ordinary taxation. Despite international pressures, Morales announced that Bolivia's infrastructure enterprises in the areas of electricity, telecommunications and railways would also be brought back under state control.

## Lessons to Learn

In most countries around the world where electricity has been privatised or deregulated, retail electricity prices have increased – often dramatically – for households and small businesses. The privatisation of power or gas was not, and is not, something that citizens have demanded or wanted. However, what is important to people is stable prices and a safe and secure supply. This is precisely what privatised enterprises very often do not guarantee. So there have been many bitter protests especially against electricity privatisation, because power providers have created artificial shortages in order to drive up prices.

Liberalisation and privatisation do not lead to more competition. In Europe, seven transnational electricity corporations dominate the market today. Three of them (Électricité de France, E.ON and RWE) control the majority share of generating capacity and retail sales in most European states, and that share is constantly growing.

A privatised energy sector is not really interested in saving energy. This would be bad for turnover and business. Neither is a privatised energy sector interested in creating surplus production capacities. This would make prices fall and this, too, is bad for business. Moreover, a privatised energy sector is therefore hardly interested in investment that does not pay off immediately or at all; indeed, this would again be bad for balance sheet results and profits.

This is why in the countries of the Southern hemisphere some 1.6 billion people, particularly the poor in rural areas, have no access to electricity; this is more than one quarter of the world's population. If no systematic efforts are made, 1.4 billion people will still be condemned to energy poverty by 2030. Today, 1.4 billion people still resort to biomass in its traditional forms (for example, wood, agricultural wastes and manure) for cooking and heating. In doing so, they jeopardise their health – for instance, through respiratory diseases contracted through indoor combustion processes. Because of the widespread overexploitation of natural resources, the time input required for obtaining fuel material is increasing, which is a particular burden for women and children.[*]

* *Le Monde Diplomatique*, 13 March 1998.

# 13

# Police and Security

Neoliberalism was 'a programme for destroying collective structures still capable of obstructing pure market logic', stated the French sociologist Pierre Bourdieu in 1998.

This becomes particularly obvious in the area of security provided by the democratic state for its citizens in numerous spheres of life, ranging from 'social security' (safeguarding subsistence levels, pensions, health systems, unemployment benefits, and so on) to security in the public space (combating crime, crime prevention, protection of public property and institutions, and so on)

For a long time, the acknowledgement of the state monopoly on violence was an indispensable precondition for the maintenance of security in the narrower sense. This state monopoly on violence consists in the exclusive right of state bodies to exert or allow physical violence. In general, this is regarded as a necessary condition for the functioning of a community based on law, also for the modern state.

In most democratic countries the police are responsible for guaranteeing public security and public order.

## Historical Development of the Police and the Local Constabulary

In early times it was the respective landlord who was responsible for security and/or it was military units that were used for security services. However, in France, a separate security apparatus was founded in 1373, which later became the model for a local constabulary throughout the world. At first, the Connétablie et Maréchaussée de France was an army corps intended for the suppression of social unrest. In the course of time the corps assumed judicial and police tasks as well. The 1536 Edict of Paris defined the monitoring of road traffic as one of its main tasks, while in 1720, under Louis XIV, this unit became the Gendarmerie de France. In the course of the Napoleonic Wars this French model was adopted in large parts of Europe, and after 1848 asserted itself in the rest of the continent. The stationing of a local constabulary brought the first regular contacts of the mass of the population with the police organs of the state, and it did not take long until its authority penetrated society as a whole. The local constabulary became the security apparatus, particularly in rural areas.

In towns and cities, the term 'police' came to be used. It is derived from the ancient Greek *polis*, which means 'town'. Since the Middle Ages the expression *gute policey* was used in German towns to describe good administration. Thus, the activities of the town administration were understood to cover all areas of life, ranging from protective to repressive tasks. To this very day 'police' in German is understood as a state organ designed to avert danger: there is also a fire police and a building police, which are not liveried troops but rather bodies competent to carry out administrative tasks.

The borderlines between administration, local constabulary, police and military units are blurred to this very day. The Italian Carabinieri as an armed force still report to the Ministry of Defence. Over the years, police have specialised in the most varied tasks. In 1829, London's Scotland Yard became the headquarters of the first specifically anti-crime police. In the nineteenth century, growing revolutionary tendencies, particularly in towns and cities, led to the establishment of state police, namely units prepared to take on intelligence and political assignments as well as counter-intelligence tasks. Another development was the introduction of border police, who became responsible for border checks as well as tasks related to customs and taxation.

## The Development of Private Security Services

The neoliberal religion, according to which the state has to restrict itself to its core tasks, is also asserting itself more and more in the field of security.

Citizens and enterprises are expected to an increasing extent to take care of their own security. These days, 'risk society' has become a common epithet. The police apparatus is subject to financial as well as personnel cuts, which means that public security tasks are outsourced to cheaper private security businesses.

Private security services assume the most varied of tasks, including such services as premises protection, concierge services, personal security and chaperoning of transports, event protection (guard and steward services), night-watch services, the installation of bugging and alarm devices, surveillance and investigation activities (private detectives), money transportation and the operation of emergency call centres; all of which have been offered for some time. The number of such services is also on the rise; they are used not only by enterprises but also, and to an increasing extent, by public institutions for reasons of economy. As a result, new tasks have been added, ranging from passenger and baggage control and the monitoring of stationary traffic to the protection of public facilities and high-ranking personalities, together with the guarding of penitentiaries and centres for detention pending deportation. Employees of private security services carry out entrance checks in public buildings and on behalf of public authorities, guard barracks and nuclear power plants, as well as carry out raids on construction sites in search of illegal workers.

Since the 1990s, private security services have experienced an incredible boom worldwide; their deployment has increased tremendously and the spheres of their application today increasingly extend into the public arena. According to estimates by Alex Vines,* the international market for private security services will grow to over US$200 billion by 2010. In this process more and more military tasks are outsourced to private service providers. In Canada and Australia, there is one police officer for every two private security officers, while in highly perilous societies such as Russia or South Africa, that ratio is sometimes as much as 1:10.

In the USA, the private security service industry is the second fastest growing business (8 per cent annual growth). Private security services are among the most profitable businesses in the country. For every single police

* Alex Vines, 'Mercenaries and the Privatisation of Security in Africa in the 1990s', in Greg Mills and John Stremlau (eds), *The Privatisation of Security in Africa*, Johannesburg, 1999.

officer there are already three private security guards, and in California the ratio is 1:4. There are 554,000 police officers in the USA, while private security services employ about 1.5 million people in more than 10,000 enterprises. Americans annually spend US$40 billion on public security, but as much as US$90 billion on private security services.

The private sentry and security business is also flourishing in the European Union. According to reliable estimates, about 600,000 people were employed in almost 10,000 security firms within the EU15. The ten new member states of the European Union added about the same number of enterprises and employees when they acceded in 2004. In the UK and Luxembourg, the number of people employed in private security services in 2000 was already higher than the number working for the police. Similar trends are seen in Germany, Finland, Sweden and the Netherlands.

Increases are expected to be enormous in Eastern Europe. In Poland, where the private security business is firmly in the hands of former police, military and secret service officers from the communist era, more than 200,000 people work for private sentry and security firms. In Russia, the number of private security firms and security services has already reached the 23,000 mark, and boasts more than 600,000 employees. The annual growth rate in this sector stands at 23 per cent, which is something of a new record.

The situation in most developing and threshold countries is similar.

In Africa, according to reliable estimates, there are already 2,000 security firms in Kenya with some 50,000 employees; here, too, the sector is among the fastest growing. The biggest enterprise is Securicor (now Group 4 Securicor) with nearly 10,000 employees. Between 1,200 and 2,000 firms employ more than 100,000 people in Nigeria, a country in which the security sector ranks second to the oil and gas industry, with which it closely cooperates. In South Africa, about 200,000 people work for more than 3,200 security firms.

The situation in Latin America is no different. In Chile, the private security industry has practically rocketed, exhibiting annual increases of up to 20 per cent and employing over 55,000 people in over 1,300 companies.

The more unsure the times are – and neoliberalism adds to this – the greater the demand for 'security', whereby the feeling of constantly growing insecurity is often exacerbated by populist political drives and media campaigns. Indeed, this stimulates business in the security industry and makes ruling and controlling easier.

The private security business therefore has enormous economic potential. The global market leader is the Danish–British company Group 4 Securicor, which emerged in 2004 after the merger of Securicor and Group 4 Falck. Group 4 is represented in 108 countries across all continents, and employs 360,000 people worldwide. In 2004, the company had a turnover of £3.8 billion and a profit of more than £210 million. The Swedish company Securitas has more than 235,000 employees in more than 30 states (mainly in Europe and North America), with sales amounting to over 59 billion Swedish krona and a profit of almost 4 billion krona. One of the largest US companies is Brink's Company with its head office in Richmond, Virginia, and 45,000 employees in more than 130 countries. In 2004, the company's turnover amounted to US$4.7 billion, while its profits reached US$120 million.

Private security providers increasingly characterise and control the public space. According to estimates, already more than 10 per cent of all private security services are active in public places, which increasingly turn into the private domains of their respective customers. These are frequently enclaves of upmarket consumption such as pedestrian zones, shopping malls and multiplexes, but also railway and underground stations (with their 24/7 shopping facilities). After all, the use of modern surveillance instruments (video cameras and monitors, light barriers, motion detectors, and so on) means that 'security' is ultimately nothing less than the uninterrupted surveillance and control of all areas of human activity.

The growing activities of private security firms are interpreted by many critics as processes that undermine the state monopoly on security and violence. There is the danger of losing the state monopoly on violence, while others hold the opinion that the power of the state would even be expanded, complemented and strengthened by private security firms, technical surveillance equipment and other new forms of control.

In any case, the privatisation of security leads to an unequal distribution of security. After all, well-to-do persons and groups who have influence in society can better satisfy their security needs. In the USA today, 30 million people live in residential areas that are guarded by private security services. There are even the first cases of social housing being monitored by private security firms because lower crime rates mean higher public grants. This development gives rise to communities of low-risk population groups. The 'right' to remove certain disagreeable people from public parks or business centres complements this development.

As a rule, private security services have no specific powers to intervene. Like all other citizens their rights are exclusively restricted to asserting the so-called rights of every citizen – that is, self-defence, emergency assistance, sanctity of the home, and so on. Although private security firms are not allowed to assume sovereign functions, time and again they take over such tasks. In Germany, cooperation between police and private security firms has been close for some time. Their joint missions range from the coordination of patrols with regard to place and time, to actual joint patrolling. In some German towns and cities, private citizens receive crash security personnel courses to become auxiliary policemen. These individuals are then employed to patrol residential areas and shopping streets in order to increase the 'subjective feeling of security' of the population at large. This development is promoted by the high number of former police officers working for private security companies. In some countries, policemen are therefore no longer allowed to work in private security immediately after quitting their job with the police.

The private security industry is a good example of a new economic service industry that is based mainly on poorly paid employment and precarious work relationships. After all, in many countries, the cheapest-offer principle is applied when awarding public contracts. Many countries also lack appropriate provisions for private security services. Sometimes this leads to grave shortcomings in the recruitment and training of personnel, in the working conditions for their employees, and in the control of the business by the state. Low pay, long working hours and excessive demands on technical skills often result in dissatisfaction, stress and over-reaction. The authority of the uniform is abused to assert a subjective sense of justice. There are often reports about resentment and 'Rambo-style' methods used against marginal groups (drug addicts, the homeless, and so on) and foreigners.

Modelled on the Anglo-Saxon experience and now also existing on the European continent, privately run prisons are booming, which also gives cause for concern. This development is alarming because less money is spent on further training and reintegration programmes for prisoners, which reduces their chances of being reintegrated into society. Nowhere else has privatisation in this area proceeded as far as in the United States, where about 2 million people are imprisoned – with annual growth figures of 3-5 per cent. More than 12 per cent of the prisoners in federal prisons, and about 6 per cent of the prisoners in state prisons, are guarded privately – and this trend is rising. In some states (such as Texas), the number already amounts to about 50 per cent.

## Prospects

With much effect in the media, and mostly uncontested in their arguments, the security industry lobby demands that 'overburdened police forces' should restrict their activities to the core business; that is, investigation. All other areas should be covered by the private security sector. In making such demands, advocates of the further privatisation of security tend to overlook the serious problems involved; for instance, the fact that private security services in contrast to the police do not act in the interests of the public, but rather pursue the interests of their employer. More criminal acts and more insecurity are good for business. After all, the new security experts are merely technicians, no longer idealists. If for no other reason, a reorientation towards the roots of criminal policy in the era of enlightenment, which focused on prevention and reintegration, would be desirable. However, as long as neoliberal elites and monetarists control the public budget policy, a change is not to be expected.

Numerous shortcomings and a lack of legal regulations in many countries have triggered an intensive dialogue between the bodies representing the interests of those concerned.

# 14

# Culture

## The History of Public Cultural Services

In Europe, the first public library was established in Athens in the sixth century BC. The most important library of antiquity was situated in Alexandria, while the first library in Rome was founded in 39 BC. In the Middle Ages, it was generally the monasteries that amassed collections of texts; their educated monks preserved and copied old books and ancient manuscripts, thus saving them from oblivion. But owing to its Index of Forbidden Books, the Catholic Church, in particular, did not contribute much to the dissemination of knowledge. The revival of ancient studies during the period of humanism promoted the zest for the collection of books, while the printing process facilitated their production. After the abolition of the monasteries in the sixteenth century, itself a consequence of the Reformation, their libraries devolved upon towns and cities, churches or sovereigns and scholarly institutions. As a result, these precious treasures were again used in a broader and more public milieu. In addition to scientific libraries, increasingly more public libraries came into existence towards the end of the nineteenth century. The town citizens were offered classical literature, fiction and specialised books free of charge or against a small fee.

The beginnings of public theatre were motivated by religion. In early antiquity, magnificent buildings were used as scenes for the presentation of the state religion, ranging from formal to theatrical. Greece was the first state to offer public space to the audience. In Rome, too, public spectacles constituted an important part of culture and rule – according to the Roman poet Juvenal, it was 'bread and games' that the people wanted. In the Middle Ages, the population was primarily engaged in amateur plays that depicted the death and resurrection of Christ. It was in the sixteenth century that humanists discovered the didactic value of theatre; at the same time plays were also used as a propaganda tool of the Reformation. The seventeenth century saw the emergence of commercial theatre companies, performing the first operas. Finally, in the nineteenth century, large town theatres, provincial stages and state theatres were physically established within edifices used to extend the fame of the respective ruler.

Museums often developed from princely 'wonder' cabinets and art chambers or special art collections. At the end of the seventeenth century, Kiel in Germany became the first town to open a public natural and cultural history museum. The British Museum, founded in 1753, is also regarded as one of the oldest museums in the world. It was primarily during the nineteenth century that public museums became established in numerous European towns and cities.

## Europe: Culture as a Public Service

In Europe from the nineteenth century onwards, culture has been seen as a public endeavour, even as a 'service of general interest', where market and competitive principles do not lead to an improvement of the service. The EU Ministers of Culture and Education are of the opinion that culture and education should be maintained and promoted as a public asset. Nevertheless, some states (such as Germany, Austria, France, Finland and Sweden) have a high density of public cultural institutions, while in others (including the UK, Portugal and Spain), private sponsorship and foundations are predominant.

Culture as a 'basic provision' means that a wide variety of cultural activities and initiatives are continuously provided in disparate fields of artistic endeavour, for large sections of the population and at prices that are affordable. Such an offer obviously encompasses theatres and concert halls, music and art schools, libraries, museums and socio-cultural centres, but it also includes appropriate forms of promotion for young artists in particular (studios, scholarships, and so on).

The official goal of European cultural policy is to maintain and promote cultural diversity in Europe. This is laid down in both the EC Treaty and the EU draft Constitution. According to the principle of subsidiarity, the manner in which cultural policy is shaped is up to the individual member states. In the event of unbridled privatisation, the Ministers of Culture fear that the focus would be on that which is 'popular' and is 'likely to attract large numbers of people' and where any type of critical culture would very soon be prevented. The end game of any such development would be marked by a worldwide levelling of culture and education in line with globalised criteria of multipurpose utility.

However, commencing in the mid-1980s and escalating in the 1990s, cultural facilities were privatised in many EU states. In the 1980s the UK began to turn its national museums into trusts that had to raise finance independently of the national authority. In Antwerp, Belgium, the renovation and further management of the town theatre was placed into the hands of Music Hall, a large cultural group. In Greece, the Greek National Theatre and the Greek State Opera were transformed into private-law societies (that is, they would operate under private company law rather than public enterprise law) in 1995.

Over recent years, numerous towns and cities in Germany have taken measures to economise, mostly at the expense of culture. As a result, many municipal theatres and libraries are threatened with closure. Museums cannot buy new works of art, they are forced to reduce the number of exhibitions organised and at the same time they have to increase entrance fees. A number of museums that had been financed by the state were transformed into foundations subject to private law. The sale of Berlin's Theatre of the West to Stage Holding, the Dutch musical group, in 2002 shows that so-called global players are also increasing their influence in the field of culture. For Stage Holding, which owns eight theatres in Germany, Germany has become the most important market in addition to the UK and the USA.

A 1996 Italian law transformed 13 national opera houses into foundations subject to private law. Using tax incentives, local pressure and profitable business prospects, the state turned to banks and industrial associations located primarily in the north of Italy to acquire interests in these new foundations. Public subsidies were cut drastically. In 2002, the Berlusconi government adopted a law on the privatisation of public cultural facilities. Subsequently, numerous properties were sold – above all historic villas to international investment companies.

The takeover of theatres, opera houses and concert halls by private foundations has caused employees throughout Europe to lose both their job security and some of their rights as employees.


## The USA: Promotion by Private Commitment

The US model for the promotion of culture is predominantly based on private commitment. Still, in the 1980s many observers believed that the European and American models of promotion would meet halfway. On the one hand, since the early 1960s, public funds designed to promote culture in the USA had been increased in an unparalleled way, while in many European states the significance of private commitment was steadily rising.

However, this development was only short-lived. In the USA, institutions for the public promotion of culture came again under massive pressure in the 1990s, when the funds for the National Endowment for the Arts (NEA) were almost halved. The NEA had been founded in 1965 as the only federal-level public US institution for the promotion of arts. As a consequence of these cuts, the existence of numerous cultural institutions was threatened.

In recent years, demands for abolition of the state promotion of culture have met with increasing political support. One of the reasons for this was the fact that in Europe the system of public subsidies also began to be called into question. One strong point of the American system was overlooked: the effect of publicly funded cultural institutions on private sponsorship. After all, the establishment of the NEA created a 'matching fund system' whereby every private donation to the arts was matched by a public one of at least the same amount. Indeed, it was the systematic development of commitment to public promotion in the USA that really gave a boost to private sector involvement. Prior to the creation of the NEA, only 3 per cent of charitable funding had been for the arts, while this amount had grown to almost 12 per cent by 1981.

However, the influence of private sponsorship on decisions relating to art can sometimes be significant: Texan oil billionaire Sybil Harrington had donated US$30 million to the New York Metropolitan Opera on the condition that opera productions should be in traditional style. Her heirs later sued the opera house for US$5 million because an opera by Wagner had been produced in a modern style.

## Culture as a Commodity

The commodity nature of art and culture is not only increasing, it is coming increasingly to the fore. Quantity – measured in audience and attendance figures ('the number of people reached') – has become the most important yardstick. In the neoliberal context, culture has also become a marketing instrument to improve the image and the marketability of towns, cities, regions, countries and enterprises. The generous donation by a bourgeois society in past centuries has been replaced by the triumphal exhibition of private property, the private museum in key urban locations.

## ... and the Reason Why Public Funding of Art and Culture is Indispensable

By definition, cultural facilities cannot be managed in a commercially profitable manner if the maintenance of diversity and quality together with broad access for all interested layers of society remain priority goals. Sufficient public funding is the only reliable guarantee that publicly financed cultural institutions not only serve the popular mainstream but also promote and present innovative forms of art which are not yet established and which may not be so popular. In most states, cultural institutions are, in fact, subject to ever increasing privatisation pressure, primarily because of the crisis faced by most public institutions. Private sponsorship may thus substitute for public funding in certain areas where cultural institutions are able to attract funding from increasingly powerful commercial interests.

Cultural institutions, associations and foundations preserve works of art and cultural monuments and present them to a broad public as well as to connoisseurs and experts. They produce music, dance or theatre, promote artists and/or art projects, and thus offer manifold possibilities to the public to participate in cultural life.

The 'basic provision' of culture to all citizens is a precondition for a democratic-pluralistic society, and this applies to the freedom of the arts in much the same way. It is no coincidence that the Universal Declaration of Human Rights, the International Covenant on Economic, Social and Cultural Rights, and the Convention on the Rights of Children all guarantee the right to art and culture. Only the public funding of culture can manage to secure a comprehensive basic cultural supply and broad access for all strata of society, and can guarantee the artistic freedom and independence of those who are active in the field of culture. As a rule, the higher the level of public funding, the better the access to culture for all those who may be interested.

Freedom of opinion, freedom of the press and freedom of art are considerably more than mere freedom from censorship. Active support by the state is required to counteract the emerging control of cultural markets by internationally active oligopolies.

There is also close interaction between cultural policy and educational policy. When dealing with art and culture, cultural education is indispensable. Conversely, key qualifications like language competence, creativity, innovative power, ability to work in a team, networked thinking and identity formation are all imparted and developed through dealing with art and culture. Therefore, art and culture make a considerable contribution to the development of the ability to live in a democracy. It is in particular the confrontation with resistance, the implausible, that sharpens one's senses and one's consciousness and awakens sensitivity in dealings with other people.

Thus far, privatisation in the cultural sector has led to the closing of facilities, and thus to a diminution of that which is on offer, as well as to higher admission prices and increased superficiality through commercialisation.

In addition to the maintenance and/or development of cultural infra-structure, the safeguarding of work and utilisation options for artists is also an urgent problem. After all, the social and economic situation of many people active in the arts is still shamefully low compared to the relative prosperity of people in other sectors in industrialised societies.

# 15

# Public Services and Unions for Women

'Woman is born free and remains equal to man in rights', stated a 1791 declaration by Olympe de Gouges on the rights of a woman and citizen in revolutionary France. The Age of Enlightenment sought an end to a millennia-year-old role concept in society. However, it took until the second half of the twentieth century before women became really equal to men, if only in progressive states. Public services played a key role in this development.

## Public Services for Women

Today around the world, women do most of the household and family work, ranging from fetching drinking water and fuel, to educating and taking care of children and the elderly. As early as 1995, the value of unpaid women's work was estimated by the UN at US$11 trillion annually.

In Africa, 90 per cent of women and girls are busy with procuring firewood and water, work that takes about five hours per day and prevents them from going to school or engaging in paid employment. Thus, in this context, the development of a functioning potable water supply is also of high social relevance because it enables women and girls to gain access to education and the labour market. Public services make a decisive contribution in improving the quality of life for women, and their opportunity to lead a life of their own with equal rights.

Owing to the advent of paid work for women and the emergence of the workers' movement, the work of women became a political theme that continues to raise many questions to this very day. Women continue to face problems that men do not, problems that men are hardly even aware of:

the compatibility of work and family, maternity protection (for example, employment protection during pregnancy; pregnancy leave; maternity leave; entitlement to relevant pensions/social security), which is still poorly developed in many countries, the interruption of a career due to the education of children, education and training of a lower quality, lower payment and fewer career opportunities for women even when they may have the same qualifications. At the same time there is also a greater threat of unemployment, and other risks such as sexual harassment. Moreover, women are often employed in those sectors where there is little or no trade union protection.

In many instances it has been public services that have made it possible or easier for women to work: by means of childcare facilities, schools that take care of children after school in the afternoon, public transport, and healthcare. The public services sector created safeguards for working women in situations that were decisive for their existence, such as in the event of accidents, unemployment, childbirth and care of children, death of a partner, or old age.

Maternity protection and maternity leave, for example, make a decisive contribution to the health of mothers and children. However, only one quarter of all states worldwide offer comprehensive maternity protection which meets the requirements of the UN Millennium Development Goals, and ILO Convention 183 which is at least 14 weeks' paid maternity leave at at least two thirds of the pre-leave income, which should be paid either by the social insurance scheme or the employer. About 600,000 women die needlessly each year from preventable complications that arise during pregnancy or childbirth, and some 18 million suffer from chronic disease or disability following childbirth.

The call for maternity protection has always been among the most important demands by trade unions. PSI provides special support for maternity protection campaigns. Those regions in which midwifery and healthcare are made accessible as public services are characterised by a significant decrease in mortality rates for both children and mothers.

The only economically developed countries that do not have paid maternity leave are the United States, Australia and New Zealand. In the countries of Central and Northern Europe in particular, there is not only maternity leave but sometimes also paternity leave or long-term parental leave. In addition, Europe offers widespread qualified institutionalised childcare that is also available for infants and is predominantly financed by the state.

Public service providers also became important employers of women. Historically, the public sector has had smaller gender and racial wage gaps, better overall pay, and higher numbers of women at professional levels than the private sector. Furthermore, the public sector is characterised by a higher proportion of managerial and professional jobs for women than the private sector and it also has substantially higher union density, which translates into greater job stability and due process rights.

In all, from a policy standpoint, there is good reason to be concerned about the continuing call for leaner government and the contracting out of as many public services as possible because women depend disproportionately on the public sector – for jobs that pay a living wage and for services that make life easier. Privatisation and liberalisation of all that public services of general interest provide for the most part threaten the jobs of employees with few or no qualifications – usually women and female migrant workers. The withdrawal of the state from the public service sector means that women will be pushed back into unpaid household work.

## Gender Mainstreaming and the Empowerment of Women

Gender mainstreaming became a worldwide strategy in the aftermath of the Fourth World Conference on Women held in Beijing in 1995, which led to a revival of the debate about the position of women in society. The purpose of gender mainstreaming is to include gender concerns in all areas of policy. The varying effects of political decisions on the gender-specific life situation should be taken into account. The strategy is based on the assumption that certain measures have a different impact on men and women. Thus gender mainstreaming recognises that all decisions can have a different and unforeseen impact on women.

Public services play a decisive role in this area too. PSI fully supports gender-mainstreaming initiatives and wants to ensure that public services serve to promote equal treatment and opportunities for women and men. For this reason gender mainstreaming will in many cases require the reorganisation of decision-making processes to ensure that measures that have been planned or realised take into account, and avoid, discrimination.

In contrast to gender mainstreaming, empowerment is a concept that is intended to achieve gender equality by means of bottom-up processes on a social basis. Empowerment addresses members of groups that social discrimination processes have excluded from decision-making processes through, for example, discrimination based on race, ethnicity, religion or gender. Empowering women is working toward helping them gain the kind of control of their lives that men enjoy, getting them equipped to take part in and influence decision-making processes. Here the primary issue is the organisation of women, to promote changes in society. It is a model followed by trade unions all over the world, but especially in countries where gender imbalances are still very strong because in these states a gender mainstreaming process based on any top-down approach is unlikely.

## Pay Equity

The demand for equal pay for equal work is one of the oldest trade union demands. The origin is, however, related to the fact that in the nineteenth century women were seen as wage dumpers* and competitors in the labour market. British and French trade unions, for instance, demanded equal pay for women as a precondition for being allowed to organise themselves in trade unions.

Women still receive significantly less pay than men for work of equal value, and in some instances are not paid the same rate for the same job. The income gap differs worldwide and is smallest in those countries where trade unions are strong and successful.

The pay gap is lower in the public sector because it is often characterised by the principle of 'equal pay for work of equal value', but only if women

---

* 'Wage dumping' occurs when a policy, such as bringing in low-paid temporary workers from a developing country for a building contract, results in downward pressure on wages for host-country workers.

reach the same positions and do not reach a 'glass ceiling' prior to that. Even in 'progressive' states the proportion of women decision-makers remains very low in the public service sector.

In 2002, PSI launched the 'Pay Equity Now!' campaign globally, and in this endeavour was supported by trade unions on every continent. The purpose of the campaign has been to make the problem of differences in income based on gender a greater priority for the trade union membership – and the leadership. The primary goal is to raise awareness of the fact that a living wage is a basic human right, and by means of demonstrations, workshops, leaflet campaigns, meetings and conferences, women's organisations and trade unions are drawing attention to the existing pay inequalities.

The campaign has already given rise to numerous changes. Some quick illustrative examples: in Ecuador, it resulted in setting up a tripartite committee to review pay and terms and conditions of work in government agencies and in healthcare; in the Philippines, there is also a pay review conducted by the Civil Service Commission; at the beginning of 2006 the Supreme Court of Canada took a decision in favour of a trade union that proved that Air Canada discriminates against female flight attendants; a comparable case in Britain involving the UK Prison Service resulted in back-dated higher wage payments.

## What Trade Unions can Do

It is still a major task of the trade unions to raise awareness of the discrimination against women in society by means of campaigns to improve their working conditions. The issue is equal pay and awareness that the work of women (paid and, above all, unpaid) has the same worth as that of men.

The advantages offered to women by the public service sector must be defended against all privatisation efforts. Trade unions have to communicate to the broader public the negative impacts of privatisation on the life of women in particular.

As women are often under-represented in trade unions, PSI decided at its 2002 congress to establish gender parity in all its decision-making structures, and this is a model that should be followed by all trade unions.

# 16

# A Growing Need for Public Services in the Future

The history of public services has proven that they have decisively improved people's lives, while the privatisation of these same services has not improved lives but has often led to their deterioration. Loss of quality, price increases, more difficult access for vulnerable groups, dismissals, wage cuts and precarious working conditions have all been consequences of liberalisation and privatisation. And neither has economic development substantially improved. The British experience with privatisation has shown that it produced no significant improvement in economic performance – as regards output, labour productivity or total factor productivity. The annual growth in productivity within the EU was more than double that of the USA both before and after the opening up of European electricity, gas and water markets.

## Fighting for Public Services is …

### *Fighting Against Powerful Opponents*

We are witnesses to a battle for the maintenance, expansion or destruction of public services; indeed, their very future will depend on the commitment and successful endeavours of those to whom public services are important.

Powerful international organisations, such as the World Trade Organisation (WTO), which was founded in 1994 to push for unrestricted global trade in commodities and services, are participating in this battle. All WTO trade agreements require that foreign suppliers must be treated no less favourably than domestic suppliers. There are agreements on trade in goods (General

Agreement on Tariffs and Trade – GATT), services (General Agreement on Trade in Services – GATS) and in intellectual property (Trade Related Aspects of Intellectual Property Rights – TRIPS). What does not exist thus far – and what PSI is fighting for – is a General Agreement on Public Services (GAPS), the aim of which is to promote quality public services based firmly on rights, and to underpin national and local democratic accountability with international standards.

The free movement of people, goods, capital and services are four basic principles that are also upheld by the EU. Since the 1980s, numerous EU directives have opened the public service sector to private providers.

Other powerful organisations that are currently forcing the pace of privatisation are the International Monetary Fund (IMF) and the World Bank. Both these bodies were established in 1944 to manage the balance of payment difficulties of states, get exchange rate fluctuations under control and finance important projects. However, the grant of financial aid is regularly linked with demands for public expenditure cuts and the privatisation of public services and state-owned enterprises. The interest to be paid on such financial aid makes poor countries still poorer, while 'donors' get richer and richer. But 'taking away support from the poorest people in the very poorest countries is killing people, says UNICEF', according to PSI General Secretary Hans Engelberts in an unpublished PSI generic speech. Instead of contributing to stability, such measures give rise to even more serious crises. The powers that control the IMF and the World Bank do not concern themselves with trade union rights or the well-being of the people. So, public services vital to the life of people are ruthlessly exposed to the greed of multinational groups and stock market speculators.

The 'other side' is made up by organisations where workers' representatives have a voice, such as the International Labour Organisation (ILO). Founded in 1919, this UN organisation specialises in the monitoring and assertion of social justice and the international recognition of human and labour rights. The ILO formulates international labour standards in the form of conventions and recommendations, setting minimum standards and requirements. This includes freedom of association, the right to organise as well as equal opportunities and treatment.

Trade unions obviously take the side of workers and also, often, of the general public. One of the most immediate challenges is the appalling attack on trade union rights that continues in many countries. We constantly hear of new violations, arrest, torture and murder committed against our fellow-trade unionists. Union organisers in many countries still put their lives and those of their families at risk. According to the former International Confederation of Free Trade Unions (ICFTU) – now the International Trade Union Confederation – multinational companies are the biggest violators of trade union rights. The most dangerous region for trade unionists is Latin America, in particular Colombia; and in Africa, too, a more and more aggressive stance is today being taken against trade unionists. Even in Europe many governments and employers are trying to intimidate trade unions and employees.

Neither trade unions nor the ILO are able to compensate for the loss of a husband, wife or parent. They can protest, they can call for the guilty to be found and brought to justice and they can keep on campaigning with the aim of ensuring that working people are not kept down by fear.

Trade unions are fighting a global battle for quality public services and services of general interest. The liberalisation and privatisation of public services has resulted in clear setbacks for workers everywhere. As privatisation is a policy pursued by international organisations and companies, trade union work also has to be international. Organisations such as PSI organise contacts and further the exchange of opinions of like-minded public sector workers worldwide. They provide arguments and represent trade unions in international organisations. If trade unions want change, they must cooperate internationally, unions in the North and the South, from developing and industrialised countries alike. They must pursue the same goals, pressing their governments to follow constructive and complementary policies. They must engage in the struggle together, and PSI is a vehicle to that effect.

As representatives of workers, trade unions must demand that as true social partners they be included in all major macro-economic planning and decision-making. Or as Hans Engelberts claims: 'Public sector unions have to be part of these debates, in the union movement and in governmental and intergovernmental forums.'* PSI therefore also calls for an alternative strategy for the public sector, in which the people are not excluded from decision-making.

## Fighting for Democracy

One goal of privatisation policy is the erosion of democracy. The public are to be deprived of increasingly more decision-making opportunities as well as participation in important areas of life. Their actions and decisions are to be replaced by those of international companies, which exercise not only economic but also political power. People are kept in constant fear of their economic security, thus making them 'willing' tools.

Powerful groups/companies, in particular, are pushing economic democracy ever further to the background. Economic democracy involves investment decisions, restructuring of work as well as methods relating to the provision of services. It calls the unrestricted right of management to manage into question. After all, many problems faced by workers are due to poor management, and in the public sector in particular public sector trade unions should clearly voice their demand for good management.

There is a tremendous lack of democracy in many large commercial and financial organisations. Therefore, when trade unions fight against the power of these groups/companies and economic control, they are at the same time fighting for more democracy.

An increasing number of people expect that global movements of citizens rather than states will be able to carry out a democratic reorganisation of the world. The trade unions can and must be part of this reorganisation.

## Fighting Against Poverty

One quarter of the world's population has no access to clean drinking water. Every three seconds a child dies of an avoidable disease. The reasons

---

* See 'Public Services in a Globalised Economy: The PSI Alternative Strategy Revisited', 1999, a publication in the *Policy, Practice, Programme* series.

for growing poverty in the world are closely related to inadequate public services. On paper, everybody is committed to the war against poverty. Even the World Bank's 2000/01 World Development Report stated that the creation of social security would have to be a priority in the fight against global poverty. The European Union is also committed to combating poverty: its priorities include participation in gainful employment, access to all services such as housing, education and training, healthcare, as well as cultural and social support.

The fight for public services is therefore also a fight for the survival of people.

The growth in world population will require a further increase in public services. As a resource, water will not only become more scarce but also dirtier, and thus it will be necessary to build functioning potable water supply systems. More will also have to be done in the field of sewage and waste disposal. There will be an increasing demand for doctors and basic health services, for teachers and family planning services. After all, more education and information can put a brake on population growth. The care of the elderly will also have to be extended. The demand for energy will rise, and more energy will be consumed. Due to the rise in world population, 470 million additional jobs will be required over the next decade, and an expansion of public services can create such jobs.

In other words, public services are necessary for the world's survival; without them the world is heading for a social and ecological catastrophe.

In industrialised countries, public services turn out to be measures that enhance birth rates. Kindergartens, crèches and all-day schools enable women to go out to paid work and take care of their family at the same time; jointly, one hopes, with their partners.


## Fighting for Public Finance

The question of finance will be decisive in maintaining and ensuring the future of public services. Poor and thinly populated areas often cannot raise the money required to develop and offer public services. However, there are many possibilities to enable them to achieve this, including the following:

- Debt relief and debt cancellation will release money for the development of public services in many of the poorest countries.
- Financial balancing between poorer and richer areas of a state is as necessary as between poorer and richer regions of the world.
- Developing countries can count on additional funds if they have a functioning financial administration that ensures the inflow of revenues.

In many developing countries, large international groups/companies and investors are granted explicit tax privileges. In recent years, capital flight to tax havens has skyrocketed, to avoid the payment of taxes. It is imperative that tax privileges be abolished, and more tax justice be achieved. International tax competition has to be stopped by means of minimum tax rates to ensure, among other things, that there is more fairness in world trade. After all, free world trade is not fair world trade. In free world trade, only the strongest will assert themselves, often using unfair means. In fair world trade the poorer countries also stand a chance. Innovative tax tools such as the taxation of currency transactions (the Tobin tax, for example) may channel more money into investments in fixed assets and public goods. Environmental pollution should be reduced by worldwide payments for the use of resources, in particular for the use of water.

## Fighting for Good Public Management

Public services are poor if the state functions poorly, as well as if there is a lot of corruption and abuse of public facilities. Countries with authoritarian anti-democratic regimes that do not permit accountability have a record of overstaffing and the poor management of public funds. Reforms should not be aimed at deregulation and destruction, but rather seek to improve public service provision.

The strengthening of national capacity for public administration is one of the best measures that governments in developing countries can undertake to realise the Millennium Development Goals by 2015.

People are the lifeblood of the public service and the main source of its vitality and strength. People in public services are motivated not only by personal reward but also by a collective drive to improve their community and the community of nations.

Effective human resource management in the public sector is very important. This involves setting performance standards, selecting the best people for the jobs, attracting and training talent, supporting and developing staff, and promoting staff mentoring programmes.

It makes excellent economic sense for governments to invest in the professional development of public service staff.

Experience has shown that trade unions do not prevent the modernisation of public services but rather support the idea of good public services that make it possible to improve people's quality of life. PSI, too, promotes positive change in the public sector and is in favour of effectiveness, efficiency, accountability and working with and for the people.

The issue is not a centralistic, monopolistic state. The issue is the recognition of the strengths of a state, its necessary tasks in society, and innovative pragmatic solutions to new challenges which have one thing in common: they are to improve the living conditions of men and women.

## Experience Success

A critical and often vociferous opposition against neoliberal policies has been developing throughout the world. There have been initial victories against privatisation, often at a local level or after a service has been contracted out.

In almost all OECD countries, public spending has actually been increasing. Strong public services are now seen as an essential foundation for decent societies, supporting investments in education, research and development. Healthy and secure populations also make business more competitive. The countries with the highest levels of spending (principally in Scandinavia) enjoy strong, export-led, knowledge-intensive growth. With the right political choices, economic efficiency and social justice can go hand in hand.

## Looking Optimistically into the Future

Public services can play a key role in introducing new social development. Good public services are a stronghold against social exclusion, poverty, disease and premature death; they are a bastion of justice, equal opportunity and growing prosperity of large parts of the population, guaranteeing more education, health, mobility, better housing, environmental protection and human security. People's quality of life is not improved by their ability to choose among providers but rather by falling prices, within the context of the maintenance of reliability and quality of performance.

PSI fights for a strong, comprehensive, accessible and effective public sector that is a tool of a democratic society in a strong economy, offering democratic public services and guaranteeing a just workplace to its employees.

It was possible to overcome the Cold War. If we succeed in overcoming the war against the state and winning the war against poverty, this could be a most significant positive turn in human development.

# Appendix A:
# Facts About PSI and Key People

## Names of the Organisation Since 1907

| | |
|---|---|
| International Secretariat of the Workers in Public Services | 1907 |
| International Federation of Employees in Public Services | 1925 |
| International Federation of Employees in Public and Civil Services | 1935 |
| International Federation of Unions of Employees in Public and Civil Services | 1946 |
| Public Services International (PSI) | 1958 |

## Presidents

The office of President was created in 1920.

| | |
|---|---|
| P.J. Teyan (Britain) | 1920–1932 |
| Charles Dukes (Britain) | 1932–1937 (resigned 23 July 1937) |
| Mark Hewitson (Britain) | 1937–1939 (installed provisionally 1937, elected 1938) |
| Tom Williamson (Britain) | 1939–1956 |
| Adolph Kummernuss (Germany) | 1956–1964 |
| Gunnar Hallström (Sweden) | 1964–1973 |
| Heinz Kluncker (Germany) | 1973–1985 |
| Victor Gotbaum (USA) | 1985–1989 |
| Monika Wulf-Mathies (Germany) | 1989–1994 |
| William (Bill) Lucy (USA) | 1994–2002 |
| Ylva Thörn (Sweden) | 2002– |

## General Secretaries

| | |
|---|---|
| Albin Mohs (Germany) | 1907–1920 |
| Nico Van Hinte (Netherlands) | 1920–1929 |
| Fritz Müntner (Germany) | 1929–1933 |
| Ludwig Maier (Austria) | 1933 as acting secretary |
| Ernest Michaud (France) | 1933–1935 |

## Joint Secretaries After Merger With the International Federation of Civil Servants

| | |
|---|---|
| Ernest Michaud (France) | 1935–1937 |
| Charles Laurent (France) | 1937–1940 |
| Maarten Bolle (Netherlands) | 1945–1946 as acting secretary |
| | 1946–1954 as General Secretary |
| Jaap Blom (Netherlands) | 1954–1956 as part time secretary |
| Paul Tofahrn (Belgium) | 1956–1967 |
| W. Barazetti (Switzerland) | 1967–1970 |
| Carl Franken (Netherlands) | 1970–1981 |
| Hans Engelberts (Netherlands) | 1981–2007 |

## Secretariat Addresses

| | |
|---|---|
| 1907 | Winterfeldstrasse 24, Berlin |
| 1919 | Generaal Vetterstraat 34, Amsterdam |
| 1929 | Berlin: first at Schlesische Strasse 42, then at Michaelkirchplatz 4 |
| 1933 | Amsterdam |
| 1940 | rue de Solférino 10, Paris |
| 1945 | 5 Endsleigh Garden, London WC1 |
| | 36 Dreyden Chambers, 119 Oxford Street, London W1 |
| 1951 | 67–69 Whitefield Street, London W1 |
| 1964 | 54–58 Bartholomew Close, London EC1 |
| 1968 | 26–30 Holborn Viaduct, London EC1 |
| 1974 | Hallstrom House, Central Way, Feltham, Middlesex |
| 1983 | 45 Avenue Voltaire, Ferney-Voltaire |

# Appendix B:
# The Otto Rudolf Schatz Prints

## Otto Rudolf Schatz

Several of the illustrations in this volume are by the painter and graphic artist Otto Rudolf Schatz. Born in 1900 in Klosterneuburg, a small town to the West of Vienna, Schatz was not 'genuinely Viennese'. The family did, however, move to Vienna, when his father who ran the local post office was promoted to the position of Director of the post office at Julius-Tandler-Platz. In Vienna, Schatz attended secondary school and it was there that his artistic talent was discovered at the young age of 16. His first works of art still preserved date back to that time.

When he took his entry exam at Kunstgewerbeschule in 1918 – the School for Industrial Arts that, after a very successful development, particularly in the era of Art Nouveau, was eventually renamed the University of Applied Arts – he passed it easily and was admitted to the painting class. At the school he obviously came into contact with students of other classes and also got to know other teachers. He stayed friends with some of them – the sculptor Hans Scheibner, for instance – for the rest of his life. The relationships dating back to his student days clearly had a great influence on his personal development.

Through Franz Schacherl, a well-known architect, Schatz was introduced to the workers' poet, Josef Luitpold Stern, a left-wing writer of Jewish origin with whom Schatz was to become close friends, who in turn introduced him to the people publishing a number of left-wing periodicals with close ties to the labour movement. Schatz started working for them, at first illustrating some of Luitpold's poems but soon also contributing to the articles of other writers and journalists. When Luitpold took on the so-called 'Workers' Calendars', he transformed them into 'Workers' Year Books', with the intention of raising their intellectual standard. Their production allowed for all sorts of reproduction methods, but it turned out that the most important one was the woodcut technique.

Schatz soon proved to be a true master of the woodcut. Most of his woodcuts were in black and white with only very few coloured ones (such as the multicoloured woodcuts particularly common in Japanese art). Normally, the woodcut produces very exact edges. The black and white meet in one line thus creating the strongest colour contrast there is; that is, black and white, which at the same time represents a precise symbol for the either/or. Since the either/or in turn symbolises struggle, the black and white woodcut offers the perfect means to illustrate any kind of dispute, including, of course, the political one. Moreover, woodcuts, if reproduced using other techniques, for instance in a newspaper, lose very little of their original quality, with the result that the woodcut original and the reproduction are hardly discernible. Finally, a work of art of such intensity can be reproduced in a small space for comparatively little money and with hardly any loss of quality. It was on this account that Schatz chose the woodcut for the major part of his socio-critical *oeuvre*. His woodcuts illustrating the world of industry and labour appeared in a number of socialist publications.

Schatz also created several large 'Block Books' with both the text and the illustrations carved in wood. The most significant ones were *Die neue Stadt* by Josef Luitpold Stern (1927) and *Stimme der Arbeit* by Ernst Preczang (1928), from which the woodcuts – pictorial documents of *Neue Sachlichkeit* (New Objectivity) – were taken to illustrate this book.

Schatz was the most important illustrator of the Büchergilde Gutenberg, an independent publishing house founded in 1924 by the German printers, a trade union initiative aimed at educating the masses. After Hitler's seizure of power and the Büchergilde's enforced political conformity, Schatz was banned from publishing in Germany and from employment altogether following the *Anschluss* (the annexation of Austria by Germany in 1938). In 1944/45 he and his Jewish wife were deported to a labour camp in what is today part of the Czech Republic. In 1947 he received the Award of the City of Vienna for Graphic Art. He frequently contributed to the periodicals of the Austrian Federation of Trade Unions (ÖGB). Schatz died in Vienna in 1961. In 1978, the Vienna Künstlerhaus honoured his work with the exhibition 'Franz Masarell and Otto Rudolf Schatz'.

## Wilfried Daim

Wilfried Daim was born in Vienna in 1923. In 1939 he joined a resistance group inspired by Catholic principles and later took part in the war, during which he was wounded three times. In 1950, he received a PhD in psychotherapy and became a passionate art collector who has never ceased to strive for the recognition of the artist Otto Rudolf Schatz and the inclusion of his works in the art-historical context. With this aim, he published *Otto Rudolf Schatz* (Eisenstadt, 1978), *Otto Rudolf Schatz – Kriegsbriefe* (Eisenstadt, 1982) and wrote an epilogue about the artist for the bibliophile re-edition of *Stimme der Arbeit* (Vienna, 1999).

Daim is the author of a series of books focusing on religious and socio-political topics and on contemporary history: *Umwertung der Psychoanalyse* (1951), *Der Mann, der Hitler die Ideen gab* (1958), *Die kastenlose Gesellschaft* (1960), *Kirche und Zukunft* (with Friedrich Heer und August Maria Knoll, 1963), *Linkskatholizismus* (1965), *Christentum und Revolution* (1967), *Progressiver Katholizismus* (1967), and *Der Vatikan und der Osten* (1967).

# Appendix C:
# The José Venturelli Prints

Several of the graphics in the book are by Chilean painter and engraver, José Venturelli Eade. He was born in Santiago, Chile, on 25 March 1924, and died on 17 September 1988 in Beijing, China.

The son of an Italian exiled engineer who supported the birth of the socialism in his mother country, Venturelli inherited his father's political convictions. As a young man he belonged to Marxist-oriented movements against fascism and supported the revolutionary movements of South America.

He entered the School of Fine Arts of the University of Chile at the age of 14. He studied graphic arts. In parallel, he studied for a BA in Biological Sciences, studied botany and participated in the creation of the National Herbarium.

The tuberculosis that he contracted at 17 years of age was no impediment. He became a travelling artist, a producer of prolific work with great interpretative force. At the beginning of the 1940s, he travelled to Brazil where he put on his first solo exhibitions. On returning to Chile he worked in drawings, illustrations, engravings and stage scenes for the theatre.

In 1950 he travelled to Mexico and then to Europe and China, and finally to Cuba in 1961, where he collaborated with the Cultural Council, organised workshops of experimental graphics and worked on great projects such as the mural for the Ministry of Industries.

In 1974, after the Pinochet coup, he settled in Geneva, Switzerland. In 1986, after twelve years of exile, he returned to and lived in Chile for the last few years of his life. He died in China while preparing his definitive return.

PSI commissioned the prints in this book for the 1985 PSI World Congress in Caracas, Venezuela.

# Appendix D:
# Resource Material Guide

## Access to Resource Material for Researchers

This book was designed to be read by ordinary members of affiliated unions within PSI's membership. In that respect, the authors did not want to 'turn off' readers who would feel intimidated by extensive academic footnotes and references. However, such material is important for researchers, academics and policy-makers who want to check out the sources. It was therefore suggested by Roger van Zwanenberg at Pluto Press that:

- we produce this appendix as a guide to such research-oriented people so that they can see the approach taken by the authors; and
- we create a website with all of the original resource material on-line.

This appendix fulfils the first of these suggestions. The website <www.books-psi.org> – is a little more complex. Apart from general information about the whole book and publicity material, it also contains:

- the text of the whole book in each finally published language – at this stage, English, French, German and Spanish
- the original German version and English translation of Part One of the book, before any serious editing commenced. It is this set of original material that contains all original references and footnotes. The order (and most of the language) is the same as for the final version of the book, so it is easy enough to locate any quote/reference in the final publication in these two original documents.

What follows is a discussion by Fritz Keller and Andreas Höferl on their approach to using the resources for the book.

## Part One: Resources Used by Fritz Keller

Confronted with the demand to collect material about 100 years of trade union work by PSI and many of its affiliates all around the world within a year, I had to make a decision to concentrate on yearbooks, congress reports or similar documents, which give some overview.

But even this decision was hard to fulfil, because the Nazi troops had stolen or destroyed the whole archive of PSI up until the Second World War, when they marched into Paris. The problem was solved through a roundabout way by accessing the Arbejderbevagelsens Bibliotek og Arkiv, Kobenhavn, Denmark and the Arbetarrörelsens Arkiv Och Bibliotek (Labour Movement Archives and Library), Stockholm, Sweden. An accident made it possible to go this way: Gerd Callesen, a historian, who had produced a directory of the Nordic archives (*Internasjonale Fagsekretari-ater – Felleskatalog over historik kildemateriale fra de internasjonale fagsekretaiater,* Oslo 1986) and is now living in Vienna, helped me with translation from Danish and Swedish.

The PSI leadership had deposited some essential and useful archival documents, starting with the end of the Second World War through to the middle of the 1960s, in the Internationaal Instituut voor Sociale Geschiedenis (IISG), Amsterdam, the Netherlands. Although this collection seems to be far from being complete, this archive contains a wealth of information.

For the subsequent period, there exists a complete collection of all important papers in the Archiv der sozialen Demokratie der Friedrich Ebert Stiftung, Bonn, Germany, and Archiv der Vereinten Dienstleis-tungsgewerkschaft ver.di, Berlin, Germany. Both institutions invested a lot of time in sorting and selecting the material handed over to them by PSI. Their detailed inventory makes research very easy.

More than an impression about business as usual brought a visit to the actual headquarters of PSI in Ferney-Voltaire, France, where an insight into the current self-image of the management team was possible. This meant not only an intensive search into the functions of the leading PSI bodies – Congress, the Executive Board, various committees and working groups – but a taboo-free (and therefore productive) exchange of views about historical events and decisions as well. Seen from this point of view, Hans Engelberts and Mike Waghorne are something like co-authors of this book.

Then there is secondary literature: especially books about the history of national trade union movements, which played an important part in the organisational life of PSI; studies about the development of other global union federations, which, for a longer or shorter time, have been in close working relationships with PSI. This was all taken from the stocks of the Sozialwissenschaftliche Studienbibliothek der Arbeiterkammer, Vienna, Austria and the Verein für Geschichte der Arbeiterbewegung, Vienna, Austria. A lot of information about the economic background and about social and cultural phenomenon relevant to PSI's history is owed to the resources of these two institutions.

## Part Two: Resources Used by Andreas Höferl and His Team

For the second part, in which the history of public services is described, sources were as different as the public services are. But we tried to use as many publicly available sources as possible, so that our readers could also use them for further research.

Much statistical material we got from the United Nations: from the Statistics Division, from UN reports such as *The World Social Situation*; from UN research units such as the Research Institute for Social Development; or the European Centre for Social Welfare Policy and Research. Many of the UN statistics, reports or publications are available on the UN webinternet sites. A very useful source was also the *UN World Public Sector Report 2005* from the Department of Economic and Social Affairs.

Very useful and important was information from other UN organisations/ specialised agencies, such as the World Health Organisation (WHO), with its *World Health Reports*, and especially the International Labour Organisation (ILO), with its *World Labour Reports*, its statistics on public sector employment, its many discussion and working papers or publications on privatisation, decentralisation and restructuring of municipal and public services.

Of greatest importance were sources that came directly from PSI, such as: its annual *Reports of Activities*; the publications in the *PSI Policy, Practice and Programme* series, on water, energy, waste, health and social services; the quarterly magazine, *FOCUS on Public Services*; the PSI electronic newsletters; and information from the PSI website, <www.world-psi.org> which is available in six official languages – English, French, German, Japanese, Spanish and Swedish (as are most of the PSI publications). Many of these publications and also documents from PSI conferences – such as speeches or papers presented at such conferences – are available either on the website or from the PSI office – <psi@wprld-psi.org>, or the archives, which are either at the Ferney-Voltaire office in France or, through that office, in the Friedrich-Ebert-Stiftung (FES) archives in Germany. Also, the European Federation of Public Service Unions (EPSU) helped us with reports: for example, on social services.

Very useful were and are the many papers on specific issues for public services produced, often for PSI, by the PSIRU (the Public Services International Research Unit) at <www.psiru.org> from David Hall and his colleagues. An overview of actual developments can be found in the PSIRU *Public Services Yearbook 2005/06*. And a good introduction to the development of public services is still the PSIRU book produced for the PSI Quality Public Services campaign, *Public Services Work!*

Interesting for our research on European countries was the OECD with its on-line published documents at <www.oecd.org> – 'figures', 'fact-books' and multilingual summaries on different issues. We obtained many figures and statistics from Eurostat. We used studies on different issues concerning public services from the FES in Berlin.

The websites of those cities, regions, trade unions or organisations we mention in Part two were also useful and interesting.

And beyond all of that, we found many useful, interesting and bestselling books such as *Blue Gold* by Maude Barlow and Tony Clarke (Ottawa, 2004), describing the world's water market, or publications such as *Too Many Grannies?* published by the UK NGO, The Cornerhouse, in May 2006. And readers should take a look at the World Bank's annual *World Development Reports*.

# Appendix E:
# The Growth in PSI Membership

Media reports would have us believe that union membership is in decline, usually implying that this is a general trend across the board. It is no surprise that growth was to be found from the beginning of PSI, but that it has continued unabated may be a surprise to some.

As Part One of the book makes clear, PSI started with six affiliates in only six countries with only 44,000 members. Membership growth in the early years was very slow: by 1910, there were ten unions in eight countries; there were ten unions in ten countries by 1913.

The First World War obviously put a break on even this slow growth, and by 1921 PSI's total membership was still only 484,112. This crept up to about 600,000 by 1931, but then collapsed again as the effects of the Nazification of Germany took hold – by the mid-1930s there were only 300,000 members.

The real growth started after the Second World War. The 1945 PSI Congress saw the admission of the first non-European (USA) affiliate, bringing the membership to 1.3 million. By the end of the 1950s there were 33 affiliates, of whom 16 were from outside of Europe. Chapter 4 of the book charts in more detail the real growth spurt that characterised the 1960s and 1970s, especially the growth in the non-European regions. By 1981, total membership had reached 8 million, and by 1989 it was 10 million. Of course, 1989 saw the fall of the Berlin Wall, and the real and dramatic growth then commenced as old and new unions from the former Soviet bloc poured into PSI. Table E1 shows the growth in one year, from 1993 to 1994.

PSI annual reports after 1994 reported on this continued growth. By the beginning of 2007, PSI represented some 20 million members in 640 affiliates. Of these affiliates, 148 were in African and Arabic-speaking countries; 134 were in the Asia-Pacific region; 141 were in the Inter-Americas region, and 217 were in the European region. These affiliated unions were in 154 countries and territories (Africa and the Arabic-speaking region, 45; 25 in Asia-Pacific; 36 in the Inter-Americas, and 48 in Europe). Of these affiliates, one in Asia-Pacific was an international union, as were three in Europe.

Table E1: Membership growth in the 1993–94 period

|  |  | *1993* | *1994* |
|---|---|---|---|
| Affiliates (total) |  | 383 | 420 |
| Countries (total) |  | 113 | 123 |
| Total members covered |  | 16 million | 19 million |
| Africa | Countries | 26 | 32 |
|  | Affiliates | 85 | 96 |
| Asia-Pacific | Countries | 22 | 23 |
|  | Affiliates | 99 | 99 |
| Inter-Americas | Countries | 33 | 34 |
|  | Affiliates | 72 | 83 |
| Europe | Countries | 32 | 34 |
|  | Affiliates | 123 | 136 |
| International affiliates |  | 4 | 6 |

In many countries, public sector union membership is still climbing, especially in developing and transition countries. There are some developed countries where there have been reversals of the slumps of the 1980s under neoliberal attacks – the New Zealand PSA being an example of a growing union. When one considers that there are significant countries where union membership is still completely or effectively banned – China, many Arabic/Gulf States, several countries in Africa – it is clear that, as democracy spreads (if it does) PSI will continue to grow, even if the growth is in countries where unions are poor and need considerable political and financial solidarity support. Added to this are the countries where union membership may not be illegal but is a bad 'career move' – such as Colombia, much of the USA, and Zimbabwe.

PSI affiliates continue to face extreme problems even in developed countries, as privatisation, outsourcing and similar policies reduce the size (and therefore the resources) of such unions. It would be foolish to assume that PSI will continue to grow or that its growth will be adequately resourced, but the historical trend indicates that the peak has not yet been reached.

# Index

Compiled by Sue Carlton